Printed in Great Britain
by Amazon

44627970R00085

KING AS A
COMPOSER

USINESS OF COMPOSING
M, TV AND GAMES

L BROWN

Produced by Softwood Book

www.softwoodbooks

Text © Bill Brown, 2

First Edition

Paperback ISBN: 979-8-21

www.billbrownmusic

*quired reading for anyone serious
*y scoring for film, TV, and video
*has pulled back the curtain on the
*d video game scoring in a way no
*s a true insider's look at the craft
*edia scoring, and Bill is extremely
* that with us. This book is also
*able steps readers can immediately
*c and careers. It's far more than a
*n how to compose for the screen.
*is own personal journey of success
* which aspiring composers can
*and video games are competitive
ights the path for the reader."

hair, Film Scoring
Music

ner, Christopher Lennertz, Terence Blanchard,
off Zanelli, Steve Mazzaro, Penka D Kouneva,
dwell, Neal Acree, Lennie Moore, Michelle
 James, Ross Tregenza, Craig Dodge, Matt
Salta, Jonny Armandary, and Daniel Ciurlizza.

ONTENTS

INTRODUC

My career has been an amazing ride so
opportunity to share some stories about
as a film composer; What I've learned over t
process, the relationships, the journey collabo
to places I never thought possible. I learned
excitement and curiosity, to follow my instinc
perspective of play and taking risks, and hav
Possibly the most important thing I've learn
knowing what is just around the corner in you
day of the 'climb' upwards, because those
fondest when you look back. *(There is no 'mo*
it" in life – career or otherwise. The great stuf
are passionate about, what you set intentions
learn more about, work towards, create, and
about learning. Everywhere you look, you'll fir
is one of the most important lessons I've learn

I'll share everything I can with you abo
learned so far. I hope I can at least entertain y
wherever you are along your path.

In this book, I'll be using anecdotes from r
applicable ideas and advice about being a c
(or didn't prepare) for the totally unexpected
ups and downs along the way. It's about how
become your career and, in the end, your life's
help of some talented friends and colleagues
perspective to the book.

Being a composer is, most importantly, a
and collaborate with along the way and the w
together creating. It's about the crazy schedu
learning opportunities, the laughs and the tears
with putting everything you have into someth
on the screen, taking everything to the next

y you never thought you were capable of, or
for yourself. With no true 'rules' and no exact
t's really about the serendipity of it all and the

e. Stay open, approach each cue as play
have fun while you're doing it! Otherwise,
so, watch out for Ewoks in your studio..." –

HAPTER ONE

JOURNEY

ith film music. Yes, Star Wars and that iconic
/as like an out-of-body experience for me. The
st and so diverse in styles, with such inspired,
st couldn't get enough of it. I was preparing
oring A-List studio features, from even before
hose film scoring and performance degrees.
My career happened! (true story) I was writing
hose studio features any day, and it had this
ot opportunities to score iconic video games,
, then CSI: NY, "studio" films and more! Every
cted, and an adventure. And I'm so grateful for

my first song at 6 years old. During those
r be at the piano or building a percussion set
multi-tracking using two cheap vintage tape
ally, is pretty popular right now in ambient/

I continued along those lines all the way
home studio began at age 12 with a Wurlitz
4-track tape deck. The next year, I worked
dishes at a local Italian restaurant, just to ha
Yamaha digital reverb with four different rev
next summer, I bussed tables and purchased
Analog Synth (which is now worth eight time
and a Roland Juno-106 analog synth. I wrote a
filling up dozens of cassette tapes with mate
friends. I was transported by writing and rec
was writing, programming, and recording, e
bang on my door at 1:30 in the morning, tellir
noise playing (he was still supportive). I don't
homework, but somehow, I made it through hi

Then came Berklee College of Music. W
and such a culture shock for me, living in Bo
people. Luckily, every part of the education re
you imagine? I was in heaven. I worked on
was there, I was exposed to so many new f
composition, technology, new styles, idioms,
going there. I fell in love with modern orch
for the first time. It was such an exciting tim
Williams, Bartok, Shostakovich, Steve Rei
even saw Keith play live in Boston one year)
learned all the rules so that I could use, be
and it was so helpful to have that foundation
orchestras and needed to be fast and flexib

*pays the best interest. – **Benjamin Franklin***

e more things you will know. The more that
*you'll go. – **Dr. Seuss***

the composer I am today without that diverse
xperience at Berklee. Even the piano 'chops'
ined there in the performance program while
jor (before completing the film scoring major)
ears. I spoke at USC a couple years ago, and it
look back and share those Berklee years, and
students who are just starting themselves and
le mountain. It was truly a gift, and it was part
his book.

oment, I just want to point out how important
your career, including when you are in school!
s, back in 1996, a friend and roommate from
Academy Award-winning sound designer who
oring to his game audio division in Hollywood.
earliest scores (something for a virtual reality
iams, James Newton Howard, and electronic
n Bhatia) that I had written just a couple years
d brought me on board a couple weeks later,
aunched. Right away, I started writing demos
anies they were doing sound design for and
Clancy's Rainbow Six and DreamWorks' *The*
out of the gate. Side note: I always thought
scoring big films in no time (I think many film
n), but as fate had it, through this series of
es found me first.

a really fun studio facility on the bottom floor
ith a handful of studios that would eventually
new scoring projects came flooding in. Over
er 50 triple-A titles, both on my own and with
ncluding the first wave of Tom Clancy's game
st Recon, etc.), *Return to Castle Wolfenstein*,
Conquer: Generals, Lineage 2, The Incredible
(Marvel), and Projects for Disney, Universal

Studios, alongside music for TV commercia
exciting time for sure. And that was just the st

During my time at Soundelux DMG, I v
director named Deran Sarafian who was w
commercial and helped him with some music
spot and called me a couple years later to sc
And a few years after that, he called me to see
with the creator of CSI (Anthony Zuiker) ab
of the franchise, *CSI: NY*. At that point, hone
scoring big Hollywood studio films any time n
the business in those years served me very
excited just to get to write music every day
modern orchestral music I imagined I'd write
full orchestras, writing big, splashy, thematic
and everyone else in the gaming world. I wa
day every day doing what I loved. Then that
franchise ... Wow. I had no idea what a big de

I had never thought of writing for TV, reall
fun opportunity, so I binge-watched all of the e
a week straight and wrote 15 minutes of new
with my own orchestral/thematic style as a d
Bruckheimer's team, and everyone involved
just filmed lots of aerial footage flying over N
I had a friend at Soundelux help cut a reel t
and that footage. A few weeks later, I was s

, at times a bit nerve-wracking, at other times
, nonetheless. Little did I know, I'd be scoring
sode was an opportunity to work hard, create
ave fun, and, equally as important, learn. I'm
it.

irst season, I took a chance and moved out of
ome studio. Taking that chance really worked
azing 9 years, which included scoring more
Super Soldier, again for Marvel, *Wolfenstein*,
films! About 9 years later, I moved to a new
studio and was scoring another TV show with
Deran Sarafian and an amazing showrunner/
Dominion Season 2 was probably the most
project like that. It was epic and thematic and
once. So much fun to score! As a side note,
.. along with a good number of scoring stages
now, but with even more quality content in
There's always magic happening! That's what
start creating again … That magic that unfolds
e amazing people I've been lucky enough to
ateful.

The following are some of the questions I
getting started in composing for media.

What hard skills and soft skills are needed
You'll need to create music that sounds pro
styles. You'll need to have a project managem
your progress, and you'll need to have great '
collaborative skills), in order to connect, crea
director's vision, and elevate the project with n
work fast and address notes gracefully using
adding drama to the process. You'll need th
produce and deliver the score on time, ever
more than you promise. You'll need to use
and nurture the relationships you create, and
to promote yourself via your website and o
compelling ways, bringing your unique person
of your promotion. (In promotion, *you* are
of your music and career second.) The first
business is build trust. Building *real* friendship
of your work, is the fastest way to get there.

How should I approach film composers in
As a composer myself, I look for assistants
the same tools I use in my studio, preferably b
Mac Pro, all related tech, all sample libraries
gear, etc.). I also listen to music they've writte
might be able to offer if I need assistance
music or arranging. Then if they meet those
person to get a sense of their personality a
things are important and contribute to my hirir

There are a few ways to go about findin
the word out there on forums like **Perspect**
and Media Composers (Facebook group) an
on social media might be two ways to start
professional, interesting, and reflect who you
glance at them will help make the case that yo
to work with (see Chapter 4 and the section ca
effectively' in Chapter 6).

er forums that might help (all of which can

for

TU

**Film Scoring
Network for
Composers &
Filmmakers**
*https://www.facebook.com/
groups/2244302700/*

**Composing for the
Screen**
*https://www.facebook.com/
groups/302384305713/*

*.com/
1248/*

ors,
je
*.com/
093/*

Music & Games
*https://www.facebook.com/
groups/493227174022269/*

*.com/
4350/*

**Filmmakers
Connect**
*https://www.facebook.com/
groups/filmconnect/*

um
*.com/
ies2c/*

**Film & TV Network
Group Los Angeles**
*https://www.facebook.
com/groups/
FilmTVnetworkLosAngeles/*

um
*.com/
akers/*

**Film Scoring &
Orchestration
Applied**
*https://www.facebook.com/
groups/filmscoringpractice/*

s

*.com/
7321/*

Los Angeles Scoring Discussion Forum
https://www.facebook.com/ groups/HollywoodFTIS/

 Documenting The Score • Documentary Film Scores & Their Soundtracks
https://www.facebook.com/groups/ documentingthescore/

HOW DO I BECOME A COMPOSE

Composer Geoff Zanelli's Assistant req
This is primarily a technical job with opp
into more musical tasks over time. Many
have gone on to composing careers of their

The ideal candidate would:
- Have at least 2 years of entry-level e
  television, or video game music
- Have a great attitude, strong work ethic,
- Have a desire to be part of a small b
- Embrace music technology
- Be VERY detail-oriented
- Work well and efficiently under press
- Be a fast learner
- Be proactive as opposed to reactive
- Be a motivated, aspiring composer v
  way up
- Have a vehicle and be able to drive

The following skills, experience, and/
considered a plus:
- Cubase, Pro Tools, VE PRO
- Engineering skills (mic placement, re
  maintenance, audio cleanup)
- Finale, Sibelius, or similar notation s
- Prior experience printing stems and
- Arranging, programming, synthesis,

ns for delivery and check accuracy against

Times for delivery
audio (trimming, tops/tails, crossfades,

 to new cuts of picture
videos and dialogue/sfx/mx stems
nce for multiple rigs
ples
s of my music for demo purposes
eetings when possible
y other hospitality runs for in-person meetings
shed projects
errands
 introduced into the job as time goes on,
cussed above is consistently well performed.

proach any library music company in order

 big credits) yet, I would study what that library
create demos in their style. Then, contact their
w who you are (also that you're a composer,
ork and love it, etc.) and that you've created
isten to in *their* production style. (Have music
nd.) Then follow up in a week. If you can reach
en better. Be easy-going and excited to help
unication. Repeat as needed.

ersifying myself and working in different
 the community see me as a film composer
and design, mixing, or something else?
promotion/website/social media. If you want to
e image you communicate to the world to be
hat it communicates that you are a **composer**.
 digital calling card), first and most importantly,
 (photo) of you that communicates who you
ively and literally). You want the headshot to
confident (but not arrogant), fun/easy-going,
Directors and producers first want to know that

you are trustworthy before anything else, and
communicate that. Also, post studio photos ar
media composing, performing, and creating ne
the images/videos and music, the better. If y
design for a really cool project, include that, b
That might be confusing to a director who is us
coming from different people. If you want to be
now. 'Dress for the job you want'. Don't wait ur
'right' look, or the coolest studio. Show who y
special. Act as if you are already the composer

What should I start doing right now or in th
As you work to pay your bills, keep writing e
finding your voice. Share your journey and mu
and developers that are starting out/at your le
on the internet, going to events, screenings, etc
create friendships based on more than you wa
music with others, let your passion for compo
musical strengths, show what you love about co
music. Play. Make it fun and enjoy the proces
enjoy every moment of it in the now. A little secr
of the mountain' in this business. The top of th
achievement, and happiness happens in the wo
grind, the climb. There *is* no top. The magic is
new skills, develop your tech/musical knowled
keep writing, and keep pushing your own bou
keep pushing yourself out of your comfort z
create new friendships! Success happens whe
opportunity (meeting the right people at the r
meet, so do everything you can to be ready for

Here are some other great thoughts on co
friend Jonny at soundtrack.academy (used
Guided study is another excellent way to gi
focus. Reading a book like Alan Belkin's
& Art is a great way to improve quickly. It v
and constraints that help to push you creativ
what you're actually doing when you compos
awesome online courses that focus on film mu
   Music theory will help you. Now, I'm no
composing you should go and learn *everything*
theory. Not at all. But you should be focused

18

ı the music you are listening to and creating –
ove.

nd vocabulary of music. You can't expect to
owing lots of vocabulary and a decent amount
o master music without it.

n. Compose every single day, preferably at the
ration will start becoming a part of that routine.

ration are two vital skills and have a lot of
ho you ask. The traditional definition is that
ɡ of existing material into a new idea and
ıposition onto orchestral instruments.

n musical vocabulary, the word 'arranging' is
ɟing of music onto instruments (as in 'big band
of 'orchestration' has become so blurred with
braries and hybrid-orchestral scores. Is it still
? Who knows!

understand this is that you need to know
f you're asked to work as an 'orchestrator' for
w what to expect?

ımposing world, arranging and orchestration
stration. That means you'll need to know how
ıries and make them sound amazing (more on

er point here: you need to know music theory.
tuation to you. Somehow, a famous composer
our work and likes it. They'd like to work with
m on their team for an orchestrator. Can you
ıusic. Not if you don't understand instruments
t the gig. Sad face. Learn your fundamentals:
notation.

ıple birds with one stone (sorry, PETA) is to
ɔtated scores and recreate them using MIDI.
res, great! If not, classic orchestral scores are
Program all of the information into your DAW,
iece as a reference track, and see how closely
one another.

to get your samples sounding realistic, but
ıe instruments you're working with and about
. You'll see and hear where instruments are
y, harmony, and bass, all while getting faster
in all clefs.

A pro 'dub stage' for learning at Berkl

Music Production

It's a solid fact that composers nowadays handing the director some sheet music and mixed, and mastered by someone else. Comp of those things themselves – particularly on in mediocre composer with great production sk the gig than an *amazing* composer with *awful*

You need to work on your production skill

- MIDI programming and orchestration
- Sound design and synthesis
- Mixing
- Mastering

Practice makes 'better' (there's no such afraid!) – so do your utmost to find ways forums, watch tutorials, ask questions, and g things you'll be doing if you're brought on as a based stuff. Setting up systems, MIDI orchest rewiring, etc. It's a vital skill.

*"Simplicity is the final achievement. After on of notes and more notes, it is simplicity tha reward of art." – **Frederic Chopin***

o make friends with composers and ask them
of one of their compositions in order to have
interesting, as you'll have a blank canvas to
as it's not your own music or a famous piece.
tracks on the internet and turn them into full
thod that will teach you the most is the one we
scores and recreate them! The only downside
suming.
es with a warning, though: don't get carried
at the moment towards these absolutely
lreds of tracks, layers, doublings, etc. That's
don't feel that you *have* to do that – it doesn't
n, 'less is more'.
ment is that of buying gear. Everyone seems to
le library or plugin is going to magically make
d mixing. It won't. Practicing composing will
nd practicing mixing will improve your mixes.
est in some plugins and sample libraries – but
agic wands'.

motional first and intellectual second." –

o be interested in films/TV/games in order to
NEW?
how many composers aren't actually interested
r, focusing only on the music. It's important to
is a 'complimentary art form'. I don't mean to
ces of art that media composers are creating,
tirely on its own doesn't always have a place in
derstand how to create drama. Where should
sic can tell the audience that. How should the
jain, music has the answer.
t the 'story' that we're telling with music, and
that before working on a project. What is the
Vhat are you adding?
writing good media music is all about knowing
ion with music and which emotion you should

Self-Awareness

We're now moving into more of the 'soft skill
need to know a few things about yourself:

- Your strengths
- Your weaknesses
- Your health

Knowing your strengths is great; it helps yo
you could be working on and how to 'sell' yo
gives you the confidence to put yourself forv
weaknesses is arguably more important. If y
covered in this book and work out *exactly* wh
be one step closer to your goal – providing yo
your weaknesses isn't an excuse to say, "No,
"Well, I'm a composer, so I don't waste my tin
a reason to **start practicing**! Health is a hu
could cover entirely within this book. But you r
healthy – and it's different for everyone. Some
all night working, while others are healthier v
and awake at the crack of dawn.

You need to figure out what makes you h
composing can mean isolation, so you neec
Composing also means long days sitting at
make sure you set up your desk ergonomica
look after your spine.

Being fit, healthy, and happy will help pull
days. I know it's sometimes much easier said

"Composing music is hard work." – John W

Marketing

Marketing is an interesting concept for compo
marketing principles in my quest to help as m
as possible, but I often struggle to see how the
composers.

Paying for Facebook ads, promoting yo
to work. Blogging or content marketing *migh*
website, but is it really likely to land you many

There is one thing that I think a lot of cc

es to other composers. Having a network of
be you'll get a few scraps tossed your way at
f course, you could wind up as a composer's
your musical network should only be half of
alf should be media professionals (directors,
e on that later.
imes help is building a bit of hype around your
showing lots of 'behind the scenes' stuff on

e you're working with see that you're genuinely
king them more likely to work with you again
aborator sees that too, they'll also be more

starting out and the small projects you're
d into smaller media festivals, getting some
music in front of the festival organizers can
the crowd and get them backing you.
to remember is that presentation is important.
can instantly help someone connect with you.
amazing and is a clear showcase of your music.
to hear your music and contact you. Embed a
je and consider adding a contact form.
s who have recommended other composers
ic, based purely on the fact that they present
metimes, the fact that you know how to write
given.
, you need to make sure everybody you know
id you need to make it look like you do it well.
Elfman both got started because their friends
ctor, simply because they knew they were "in a

s 'people skills'. There are a variety of things
en it comes to working with people.
is networking. It's a skill that so many people
ard, it's uncomfortable, and that's because it
f faith. Will this person like me? Will I say the
rd?
r to those questions?: What does it matter?
reach out to someone and then never speak

to them again, you've still given yourself an i
make a connection than if you hadn't reached

There are certain 'tricks' you can learn
the simple version is this: a) don't try to se
interest in them.

> "'Just beautiful,' he said. 'Impeccable pres
> from a quick glance that he has absolutely
> **Neal Acree, quoting his college professo**
>
> "You can make more friends in two m
> interested in other people than you can in
> other people interested in you ... which is
> that the way to make a friend is to be one."

Other people skills that you'll need:
- **Coerciveness:** Not only to convince s
  is the right fit, but also to coerce music
  performances, or to convince a directo
  for live instruments will help make the p
- **Openness:** You need to be honest with
  feedback. You may not always be corre
  that. And even if you are correct, some
  trying something different can present
- **Generosity:** The more you give, the mc
  as simple as that. Help people as much
  in your career, make sure you give som
  someone else. Sounds a bit spiritual, b
  people I've spoken to have mentioned

Filtering

I don't mean filtering *frequencies* – I mean filter
is out there. There is so much content, so ma
you need to know where to start.

In terms of filtering through **what to lea**
that you like and trust. Don't try to watch/re
of information out there or you'll never get
you are finding ways to continuously improv
might be missing.

vho you're listening to as well. Facebook
to continuously learn new things through the
e also full of a lot of misinformation. Figure out
information and who's bullsh*tting.
out the projects that you should be working
out, you'll likely be looking at working for very
he golden rule with that is if *you're* not getting
g paid) – you need to decide whether a project
yes to anything and everything.
or/producer has planned for the project. Will
? Do they have a distribution plan? What's the
e they trying to get funding for another, larger
volved in, for example? All things to ask and

vork out: Does the director respect music? If
ever in working with them. Any media creator
c or who has no respect for music is unlikely to
ake sure they're actually *interested* in and have
and how music will work in their project – or
cuss it in detail with you. If they've no time for
.

work for free, and most good directors should
at and will have a budget set aside for music.
is really worthwhile just being involved in. All
bad projects!
ork out whether the financial reward (or lack
ect. A TV commercial is going to do nothing for
w – don't start ...), so you should be expecting
hort film tackling an issue really close to your
artistic expression but could also lead to other
might pay less but could be more worthwhile

v spam filter pretty effectively." – 'Weird' Al

Negotiating

Understanding the art of negotiation can help
not only with your music. One thing to unders
about 'winners' and 'losers' (at least, not the
help us). It's about working *collaboratively* to
outcome.

The following lists some things that you'll
negotiate.

The Musical Direction

You'll have to negotiate the creative directic
people. Some of those people might be extr
others might have more of a financial interest (
they'll all want to have a say, and you need to
what the final music will sound like.

The Final Mix

In the final dub – where movie, sound, dialogue
– you'll need to negotiate the music with o
worked hard at their individual parts, and ever
hard work is heard. Again, it's about collabora
best serves the project.

Budgets

Remember, it's not a 'fight' to try to get m
to work out how to best serve the project. Y
realistic discussion about what the project c
and what they could afford if they could stretc
a budget of 3-5% of the project's overall budg
or manager who can do this for you can be ve
from the 'business' side of the relationship an

Bear in mind how powerful the word 'no
way. A 'no' can halt discussions entirely. Have
plan with an *overly* negative person? Nothing
who say 'yes' are so much easier to work with
avoid saying 'no', and instead, work on solutio

"If a man will begin with certainties, he shall
be content to begin with doubts, he shall
Bacon

a basic level, you need to make sure you can
structures on your system to keep all of your
er drafts of things in case a decision is reversed.
any draft, of any cue, on any project that you've
. The last thing you need is to be opening and
d again every time you send samples to anyone.
e to manage a project. Early on, you'll likely
w, looking after everything yourself. But then
ect and will need to manage other people (like
ou step up, the more moving parts you'll have
s will be absolutely essential here.
ganized is also vital. Don't just rely on your email
itacts – create groups, address books, whatever
ny details about the person as possible. It's too
ie but remember their company, or vice versa.
n have a 'Christmas' or 'New Year' list that they
he relationship alive.
fluencer on social media, it's a good idea to
so that you're consistently sharing relevant
a weekly 'here's what I did this week' post,
a potential collaborator would love to see that
you have to keep on top of all of the platforms
ofile on – it's no good having a picture and
o on a talent site. Create a bookmarks folder
ouped – then whenever you have an update,
e and edit to make sure they're all fresh.

-employed. Being self-employed comes with a
kes and health insurance, through to contracts
e things more complicated, it's likely that your
ed, distributed, and marketed worldwide. That
complications regarding licenses and royalties.
s is that there's generally only a few different
are organizations that can help you. It's worth
AP in the US or PRS in UK – they offer lots of
ple or template contracts you can use.
d idea to have a good entertainment/copyright
your address books. Just in case, or for when
e.

For business skills, you'll need to underst

- How to register yourself (either as self-
- How tax/health insurance works in you
- The types of contracts you can use and
- The ways in which you can be paid (fee

*(Thank you to my friend Jonny at **soundtr** this chapter! Make sure to check out his site!)*

LINKS TO MUSIC MENTIONED IN T

Lineage 2
https://open.spotify.com/al bum/04wngi30Qap95fjcdn7 SbC?si=He0Z8x67QNONW XJIXIC-iQ

CSI: NY
https://soundcloud.com/ billbrownmusic/sets/tv- music-for-crime-dramas

Captain America: Super Soldier
https://soundcloud.com/ billbrownmusic/sets/ captain-america-super- soldier

Tom Clancy's Rainbow Six
https://soundcloud.com/ billbrownmusic/sets/tom- clancys-rainbow-six-the

Dominion Season 2
https://soundcloud.com/ billbrownmusic/sets/ dominion-season-2- exclusive

HAPTER TWO

OF THE TRADE

_____

ese days, you can create a broadcast-ready
top, audio interface, and some speakers and/
g about this photo of my studio is that 'most' of
the box' or in the main computer's DAW (Digital
at way because scoring for media most often
ready (ready to do as many versions as needed
dless of how simple or complex your system is,
d making sure you always have a microphone
t something live – at least one instrument or
It could be your voice, re-imagined with effects
playing something unexpected (an unexpected
litional percussion track. The more live elements
ally unrecognizable as acoustic in the final mix.
of having organic and unique sounds in the mix.

29

WHAT DO YOU NEED TO GET STAI

1. Laptop/PC – with enough power to run Log
etc., and enough hard drive and back-up drive
room to spare. Make sure your drives are alwa
is a back-up system that does this automatic
and it has saved me more than once in the
have more than 12 TB (terra bytes) of samp
system, 1 TB for my application drive, 2 TB fi
my project drive. Most newer systems use
recommend. And remember, you can never h
Just starting out, have an 8 TB drive for eve
grow. I have an *almost* ridiculous number of lit
be overkill, but who knows? Technology con
and by the time this book is published, I'd im
priced lower, and lower again the next year.

2. A **DAW** (Digital Audio Workstation) – I us
others, like Cubase, Digital Performer, Pro Tod

3. Speakers and headphones – I recommen
speakers. You want to make sure your mixes
stage so that the way it sounds in your mix er
and/or sounds as you intended in the final pr
car for another take on it. And then in your frie
something after you've put so much love and
Adam and Genelec speakers and AKG K271 r

4. A MIDI keyboard/controller – I recomm
keyboard so you have immediate access to a
without having to scroll through octaves on a s
many options these days, but in the most pr
you'll find these most commonly:

- Doepfer LMK2+
- Yamaha s90
- Doepfer LMK4+
- Studio Logic SL88
- Native Instruments 88
- Arturia 88
- Novation Launchkey 61 etc.

ynths – You'll find a pretty exhaustive list of
chestral and otherwise) in Chapter 9 under
very time I get a new library, I'll go through and
patches, and effects in it to Logic Pro's CSS
ve them broken down into folders by category:

es inside each category folder, like this:

ne for me when I sit down to write, because
h effects set up!) are right there in categories,
on a project, I'll save the instruments/patches
eir own folder (under that project's name) so I
project as well.

31

CREATING TEMPLATES

A really important part of being prepared
composer is having the right sounds ready to g
within your DAW. Sample libraries have cou
instruments to choose from, and I'm always on
It can be daunting at first because there are
good sounding versions of the same instrume
of nuts and empty your bank account if you'
instruments for a lot of the sample library co
to really dig in and learn the library so I know
online and listen to demos of the libraries to se
created with them, which can be very helpfu
changing, but the concept of creating templa
remains the same.

I have several templates saved in Logi
include my basic template with orchestra,
patches, a synth template with lots of my f
mastering template with my favorite mastering
go. I also have templates to quickly check ste
a cue, generally 8 to 10 (equal length) audio t

s in a cue, with matching start and end points.
ix stage, they equal the original mix of the cue
ed as needed for the project to the director's
mix.

to record in my templates with all instruments
stem record tracks, ready to go! You can see
how they are labeled per instrument group.
rly, I set the stem tracks to record and capture
can be a big time-saver, especially when you
ed to send a quick fix to the dub stage.
C to run my orchestra template's instruments
y main computer. That PC is tethered to the
(Vienna Ensemble Pro); software designed
The fastest, most powerful computers these
n, like the Mac Studio, but those are still pretty
good to have options.
olate I used on 'Michael Fights in the Rain' from
w *Dominion*. You can hear the final version of
- Michael's Theme' on my Soundcloud. *(See*

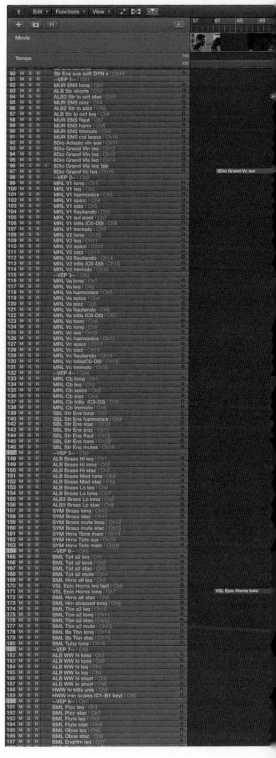

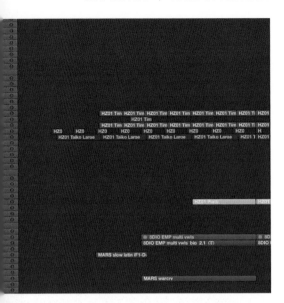

...estral template uses an updated version of these
...he Spitfire BBC Symphony Orchestra Pro, etc.)

...lways changing, but this concept stays the
...t and articulation needed to take an idea from
...st in mock-up form!

...YNTHS

All of the analog synth and modular gear I hav
part, captured as audio somewhere in the pr
when needed, whether that's before I start wo
or while working on cues in progress. Progra
can take a lot of time, and sometimes I'll st
saving new custom sounds, patches, and
The audio captured in the Logic Pro session
along with all of the internal synths and instru
and analog synths might look daunting, bu
process, it's just creative play. You start with a
oscillators, and feed that into any number of
that sound and send that to your DAW. This is
unpredictable form. Sonic 'accidents' can be
unexpected in the cue. 'Unpredictable' explor
of creation can be a very good thing.

Here's a simple explanation of the module

1. Oscillator – This is your sound source.
2. 'Shapers' – These are your LFOs, VCA
   etc., which help you **shape the sound**
   ostinatos, and **harmonic content** ove
3. Effects – These let you color the sound
   reverb, etc.) and place the sound in sp
   types.

You could leave your patch (the combin
effects) dry and add effects to the files you c
Or you can experiment with effects in you
both! Remember that dry sounds up front in
sounds that are pushed back into reverb ar
same way in your mix. 'Really big' doesn't so
subtle' before it.

Dynamics and space can be used in you
part. The contrast between dry sounds and a
into reverbs also creates dimension, and us
creates even more. Maybe the drums and bas
ambient guitars have lots but also have a hig
the vocals are almost dry with a subtle reverb
the mid-range. Each part has its own place in
through reverbs/delays. So always remember
best friend in a mix.

cially modular synths, can be time-consuming,
ue to your project/sound. It's just another way
ing original for the track. I'll sometimes take a
w textures, pulses, etc., for a specific project.
ng is happening in 'real-time', so it oftentimes
and manipulated in that form for the score. Not
s. It's a bit like driving an 18-wheel truck (stick-
utomatic transmission. And again, they're not
ls to play with. Regardless of the complexity of
creatively with it. For instance, if you give John
t that one instrument – what does he do? He
crazy-fast melodic line in Hedwig's Theme for
t that one simple instrument surprised us. *(Not
he rest of the orchestra!)* So don't worry about
has ... you can be wildly creative regardless!
er and say that finding a unique 'sound' for
re valuable than using every instrument that
et again. Some of my favorite scores are those
ments in a totally fresh and surprising way.

– my Euro-modular rack in action

My two custom-built 7u analog cv modular synths
the Moog modular using original electronics, the

synths are the easiest to program and
are so much fun to create with!

I recently built a scaled down 'portable'
The new Apple Mac Studio (currently M2/M3
composing!

This simplified but still powerfu

Mac Studio, Hard Drives, UA Volt 4|76P A
Launchkey Midi Controller, Samsung Cur
Monitor, Genelec 8030-C Audio Monitors, Ac
CP850 UPS System (power condition

...ck that holds the UPS power, Mac Studio,
...(SSD, etc.) for my semi-portable rig.

THIS CHAPTER:

...ne)
...LyP

CHAPTER THI

THE CREATIVE

*"The Universe doesn't create through hard \
flow is the mode of manifestation. Follow yo*

"It doesn't have to be perfect, just write
Billy Joel

I like these two quotes because they are rem
In the beginning, the canvas is blank. The p
you can't steer a parked car, we have to star
when and where to 'turn' (pun intended!). Bill
it doesn't have to be perfect. And it doesn't h
We have to trust that, at some point in the pro
itself to us and then just *'play'*.

It's interesting that the word 'play' is use
relates perfectly to creating it! Whether it's
minimal electronic score with a few live overdu
'playing', listening, letting those ideas come
core emotions as a storyteller and collaborato
themes, and rhythms and building a palette tha
is a process we can choose to look at as explo
feel like hard work and struggle at times, the tru
the way, explore the possibilities, and let those

Your subconscious artist, that part of y
soul, infinitely knows what works, what is need
it's coursing through a scene or gameplay. Yo
the right direction when the music surprises m
when layers that didn't exist in the unfolding
in a new way, and when I can't help but want t
been the same throughout my career. There's

he underlying rhythm of a scene or empathize
even if it's subconscious; all of it informs the
those moments when watching a great film,
game; moments that take our breath away.
genre, the music should strive to express the
n – the subtext. Imagine an action scene, for
the narrative is more about the character's
; an opportunity to play 'against the picture' in
e for that character's emotions. That's how the
by expressing what words can't express and
plain.

I'll watch the film or read the script, or with
videos of game play, watch cut scenes, play
neck out art materials from the project. While
ough the script and materials, ideas will start
ubconsciously. I'll even start to dream themes
o the studio the next morning to transcribe and
; to meet with the director or team to discuss
nce we have a collective creative direction in
nd create either a series of themes, a theme
eate underscore for specific scenes that will
e.

After I record some ideas, I'll have the dir
studio to go through the new material, or just s
out. We'll discuss the direction from there (o
my new score synced to picture), and then it'
score and repeating that creative process until
I'm working on a TV series, I'll get together
the writer(s), editor(s), post supervisor, music e
We'll watch through the episode and discuss th
detail. I usually get the 'locked' picture (the fina
the next day and then deliver the score 4 to 5
on *CSI: NY*, I would write new thematic material
and deliver after a few days of writing, recordir
and games, it's a similar process, though usua
depending on the project. With TV, 'locked' or '
is usually *actually* locked*. This is rarely the c
can have 'locked' v4, v5, v10 ..." With digital e
extend, or delete any part of a scene, they'll m
all the way up to the final dub (the final mix of
and sometimes even past it. Network TV as w
and subscription watching is the new normal.
ready to deliver, regardless of the post schedul

For this, discipline is *key*, especially whe
proactive, communicating with your team, and
way to stay on top of your game. When you're w
more relaxed schedule, it can help to take your
smaller goals, even for 'soft' goals that can be
ask yourself, "What needs to happen now? Thi
clear on how you will successfully meet your de
involve other questions. Do I need a team? An
I need to hire someone to handle asset manag
specifically) or a music lawyer to help me wit
important questions. Break it down into focus
organized by using a spreadsheet, Google doc
track of feedback from the client if needed. G
have a 'live' creative document to communicat

Another really great film music manag
(Cue Database) was created in recent years a
organizing and communicating with collabor
process. CueDB allows us to enter all cues a
the progress of each cue through all aspects

---

1   (*'Locked' picture = the final version or edit of the film/epis

rom notes to completed, prepped, recorded,
th our collaborators. A bonus to using CueDB
 your music editor can use that same CueDB
ate the project's Cue Sheet at the end of the
nt. Delivering a complete Cue Sheet (with all
on needed to deliver to the respective PRO
 agencies, i.e.: BMI/ASCAP, etc.) is super
 agencies will track and calculate any royalties
 the coming years.
ots of how I used CueDB to organize all of
of the project for one of my recent films titled

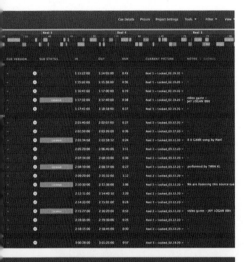

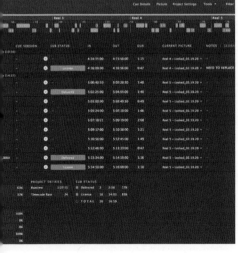

e CueDB template from Hero Mode)

(Screenshot of the CueDB template

I also use my sequence folder (sequenc
file containing all sequenced digital and audic
project) to stay up-to-date, organizing and
as 'in progress', 'sent to client (waiting for fe
stem', and my favorite one, **'completed'**, al
moving target in this business! (True story.) T
a handful of folders I use to organize all of the
You'll see in the image below how I organiz
folder. In this case, for the film *Negative*, y
each aspect of the score, including **assets** (s
notated theme books, asset management doc
sound design, rhythms, and thematic ideas p
the specific project), **mixes** (all current cue
versions ... remember to keep *everything* –
and audio formats, and keep it organized a
the mastered **soundtrack** album and rela
sequences (I use Apple's Logic Pro to crea
and save each version separately, always plac
separate folder), and **session files** (this is sp
happening on the project and can contain a
prep for orchestration, midi, and audio and cli
the Pro Tools or Logic Pro audio from the reco
a couple of folders for the music **'stems'**, wh
length that contain the separated elements c
split my cues out into at least 8 to 10 stems c
so the dub mixers and production team have
mix all of the elements together.

ll Me?
o You

anizing my sequences is green for completed!

es requested by the director or team, having
oroject can be really helpful. If the picture only
oment and you've moved on to another project,
nes edit the cue to work with the new picture
d. A music editor is also incredibly helpful to
spotting notes at the beginning of the project
g sure everything is working on the dub stage
ck(s), which you will attend, and then creating
or episode is mixed and delivered. Cue sheets
.e., BMI/ASCAP/SOCAN, etc.) for all film and
e cue type, cue length, placement, and writer/
e of music in the project.

				Netflix ID #:			
				Release Territory:			
ess: ...							
				ISAN/EIDR #:			
Music Duration:							
poser: Bill Brown				Cue Sheet Prepared by:			
c Supervisor:				Cue Sheet Prepared by (#)			

PUBLISHER	PERFORMER	TIME IN	DURATION	USAGE	SOCIETY	IPI #	Notes
PUBLISHING - BMI	Bill Brown	1:04:27	0:58	BI	BMI		
PUBLISHING - BMI	Bill Brown	1:12:47	0:43	BI	BMI		
PUBLISHING - BMI	Bill Brown	1:13:22	2:43	BI	BMI		
PUBLISHING - BMI	Bill Brown	1:14:59	1:36	BI	BMI		
PUBLISHING - BMI	Bill Brown	1:16:40	0:23	BI	BMI		

e you is to let go of attachment to the work and
e surprised if 'locked' picture gets 'unlocked'
ue yet again to work with picture or to satisfy
reminds me of the Edward Harriman quote,
he lack of a little more." Remember not to take
giving it your all. Soon, you'll have a completed

score, and your team will really appreciate h
the process. Remember that a director has
and, at this point in the process, the music ca
the months (more often, years) of complex de
they have been under.

Remember, film music is **collaborative.**
the project, in service of the director's (and
score we create has a life of its own, even ou
great. There's no guarantee of that, and for
know which scores those would be as I was
we're working on the project, we have to rem
service of the project, in collaboration. It's r
creating the best possible score, together w
our listening skills, enthusiasm, craft, patien
Stay calm, stay open, approach each cue as
and have fun while you're doing it. Otherwise

THEMES ARE AWESOME

Using themes can serve the project and your
can connect the audience, even if unconsciou
characters, a place, or a time. It can serve as
know what's happening behind the words b
even clarifying the emotion behind the action

In the summer of 2015, I met with Vaun W

ning onboard to score season 2. We discussed
ved, and we discussed where season 2 of the
conversation about scores we loved, the wide-
upcoming season, and how the score could
st night after I met him, I had three big theme
'dreamed' a few of the really important ones,
hen I start projects; ideas just start to come
great because it's a totally unrestrained, sub-
thing can happen in the shower or in nature –
ved that space, and counter-lines, orchestration
d! I just get out of the way and let it happen).
with 'Michael's Theme' and 'The Chosen One'
head and ran into my studio to get them into
s Theme over to my friend Deran Sarafian, who
ing/filming the first episode of the season, and
of 'Michael's Theme' during the filming of an
spired to approach the action score, and the
ted ways. 'Michael's Theme' is very emotional,
battle sequence to inspire the actors.
ting were part of the process throughout. I
sions of the themes and all the early ideas as
y to have a few weeks to ease my way into
create this palette of character themes and
s Theme', as I started to flesh it out, became
more complex. I added electric guitars, live
nalog synths, and more. I had about five days
metimes a little less. We weren't set up with a
estra, so I would bring in players to sweeten the
r is just me in the studio, using Logic Pro, my
s template, and synths, along with performers
llo on the score, George Doering performing
ic, and electric guitar parts (I play a bit of the
his enormous amount of experience to it that I
instrument), and ethnic winds, with Chris Bleth
ne flashback sequences throughout. It's really
ers, even if it's just a few; it adds an incredible
core.
motionally rewarding about getting to create
there's kind of a bond there. You've got this
y, "We brought this thing into existence." And
to play with an orchestra, and with the caliber

49

of players that I got to record with on that s
takes it all to the next level. It brings human er
with words but can only be felt with the hear
as composers, too. Those are the moments a
your career and your life.

When I started creating themes for *Dom*
away from picture to get started because th
was just being filmed. I was inspired by the cc
and Deran and some great pre-production ar
upcoming season. But I would recommend
start anyway! The idea being, after you've at
about the project, you can step away and let
'unconscious' artist guide your exploration.
up with in those first three weeks became
would use throughout the season. From there
craft of composition to really take advantage
then evolved throughout the season. Somet
combined or stretch out one theme so it play
Different arrangements, instrumentation, te:
creating an almost endless (but still recogni
that created connection, emotion, suspense
the season. Using themes in all of these w
experience, even if in unconscious ways for th

through the season, you'll hear how themes
'er the arc of the season. (Look for *Dominion*
(See link on Page 58)
ome music videos I did during the recording of
channel. *(See link on page 58).*

n 2 dub stage – ep201. Mix in progress.

deadline, the advice I would give is to trust
:o second-guess yourself. Sometimes, I'll hear
st transcribe that idea using the best tools at
ive, get it to work in context, and then move
h fresh ears at some point and when more
created. Also, bringing **live players** in can be
l. Even just one live instrument will breathe life
ome alive. I highly recommend it! If an idea is
a shot. Trust your instinct and find the samples
'e.

Sometimes you have to just work with yo
it. It's not all *inspiration*; that's actually rare fo
with your technical skills, don't be surprised i
(it probably will), and don't be afraid to step av
your breath if you're just drawing a blank. If ne
a walk, let go of it needing to be 'perfect' or 'gi
Don't try to force it. Instead, relax and set a
again. Get back to a beginner's mind; play
curiosity, even playfulness. Life just works bet
just with music! If you live your whole life fror
curiosity, your path/journey can be both grace

When I'm working on a cue, the **narra**
Sometimes the orchestration, arrangement, a
a cue can inform the next section. A sound, a
you discover in the process of refining can infr
And in regard to writing section to section, I
mind. The narrative will inform and inspire the
there is a point in the film (etc.) where the mo
switching to another theme I've written for the
fresh with it will serve the moment. It's always
works or it doesn't. This could include chang
instruments, a new theme, etc. If something a
most often on the right track, or getting closer

To learn about writing thematically, I high
as you listen to the recorded scores to get a
did it. One example I'd offer is Hindemith's 'F
orchestra). Get the score and a recording of th
be amazed at the **simplicity** of the writing a
the orchestra. Find some scores you really lc
out of it!

Deadlines really can be our friends as ar
become more and more disciplined with e
impeccable communication with your team ar
what is most important in your process, help
build trust at the same time. Check out this r
vs. burning out.

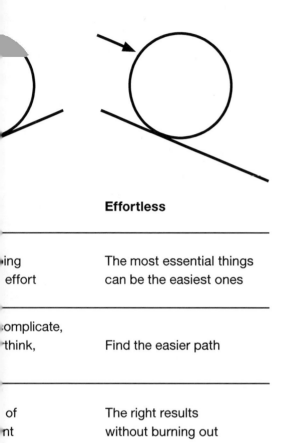

Effortless

·ing effort	The most essential things can be the easiest ones
·omplicate, ·think,	Find the easier path
of ·nt	The right results without burning out

'S BLOCK'

point as you're writing? We can find ourselves
tion of the project without inspiration, or even
blank canvas. We have to start somewhere …
'ou have to get it moving first, and then you can
music, we need an idea to begin and 'steer'.)
g, we can begin to accept the idea that there
ust a lack of beginning (for whatever reason).
about being stuck, step away for a bit, take a
·ffee, do something you enjoy. When you are
tunity to play, unattached to any *one* outcome
·ne purpose). Just try something out, listen to

53

some new sounds, learn a new piece of soft
a new instrument. Just play one cool-sound
expectations fall away. Sometimes just getti
different environments can be enough to let
that **control is an illusion**. Let go and have fu
find what you're looking for. Do or do not, ther

Setting **intentions** can also be very pow
in life in general. This could apply to how y
relationships, and even yourself. (Hint: You ca
with yourself and remember that "It's not the
you are with yourself as you go through the is
to work on your project for two hours and th
yummy food. You could set an intention to a
of mystery and wonder, with an open, playf
intention to collaborate with someone new t
forward …

Try it out! Set an intention for something l
your director, for instance. It might be someth
conversation is to listen deeply, to understand
to bring a fresh point of view to this project a
or "It is my intention to be of service to my dir
give him or her my full presence and understa
for this opportunity to connect with them".

Setting intentions is a powerful, groundi
that helps clarify your sense of purpose. You
meeting with a potential client or team. Mayb
you carry with you as you go about your day t
awareness to your interactions. For instance,
be: 1. To have fun; 2. To connect in an authe
gratitude (in whatever ways those all show up

Those three intentions served me ver
conducting an orchestra live in concert. As I
I remembered my intentions, and it was clea
there to enjoy myself, really connect with my
audience later) in an authentic way, and sh
That doesn't even cover the incredible and
I experienced during the process. But I was
I already knew I would be grateful for this e
territory for me, it was an adventure. It gave r
from mistakes, let go of the need to 'contro
anyway), and just have fun with it.

are often created so that the team working on

nse of what the project feels like with music

before a composer is hired). This happens

ames. It can work in your favor if *your* music

it's working well, they'll most likely hire you to

popular temp score or style of temp score for

was hybrid action suspense scores; five years

l analog synth sound design/acoustic hybrid

it turned to retro analog synths and the pure,

ths from the 80s. Next will probably be some

gain … or maybe the pendulum will swing all

r prepared piano, guitar, etc., and so it goes.

e person that sets the trend for the next temp

ally work in your favor!)

eer, you might be working on a project where

with the temp score. This can be challenging

advice is to be proactive. After you meet with

uite of themes/ideas for the project away from

conscious open up and pour out ideas. Don't

nd if you need to, remember you don't *have* to

. And don't be afraid to think outside the box.

mes/motifs, etc., that you feel are working for

your director or team. Don't make excuses for

y to explain what you did, because you might

ea … Just share it with them! That's it. Add a

e ideas I'm working on for the project. Let me

need to describe where you feel an idea might

theme, be brief and keep it simple. This is a

job to bring our point of view and help elevate

th the team.

t my experience working on *Dominion* Season

ng them to the director to play on set while

vn. The reason I'm referencing that story now

ck Love" is to share with you how I took the

n early by writing themes and sharing them

ney started editing the first episode, my new

way into the cut. Additionally, any temp that

y ideas was helpful for all of us on discussing

t in regard to music I would write that week

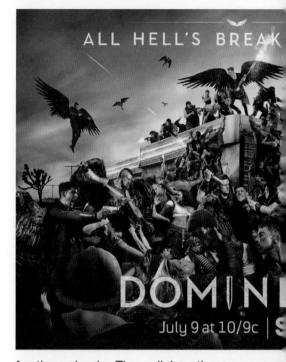

for the episode. The collaboration was easy
about what we were creating together. It was e
the creative process; challenge, inspiration, fur
a thematic and exciting score were all part o
wasn't a stumbling block, it helped us work f
easily about the direction. Many times through
used in the temp, which helped inform my nex
and the sound of the score. With my nine yea
NY, I definitely had a head start with writing
music in one week. Being proactive about the
early on helped the whole team feel more re
about the score overall.

One other thing to keep in mind, as a c
have to do what the temp is doing. Even if th
have to do that. Your job as an artist is to find t
best. (HINT: It's not always that pulsing thing
everything in the scene.) You can make a new
do it. I dare you.

Composers know what I'm talking abo
kicking ass. Of course it is! The budget for th
a million dollars; the composer had a year to v
about the idea. So, what is *your* idea? There's

core comes from the depth of how the score
sh way, and to itself internally, through motifs
atic ideas), and thematically. *(That means your*
an the temp!) Try to watch the scene without
ment. Think out of the box. Sleep on it or move
hat scene is challenging at the moment and
a comes to you (if you have time). If not, work
all the tricks and go-to ideas you've learned so
d to finding something magical!). You're lucky
r a living, so just go for it. Don't be afraid of it.
at scene is here so that you can write the best
itten, something that surprises even you!
t to write, something you're inspired to write.
re is only one *you*, so be yourself 100% and
d remember, **patience** is a super-power! And
d empathy are some of the most important
dy, especially for yourself as you go through

CE BETWEEN WRITING FOR GAMES,

iums (Games, TV, Film, etc.), I try to approach
There are technical differences in creating for
e is the same. Connecting with the narrative,
and that moment when you find the theme or
o the next level, is magical. When it happens,
starts to happen where things start to fall into
e scene or the project has just elevated and
mething new. Discovering the next pieces of
. There's something in that transformation – in
ably *why* we do what we do as composers.
t that's one of them.

E/MAIN TITLE SEQUENCE

sic most often sets the tone of the film for the
t think they know what genre the film is, but
s be a psychological thriller? Will it be exotic,
ain Title can tell a story before the *film* tells the
es introduced in the title sequence will appear
e film.

Sometimes, the Main Title just places th
of the story, creating a sense of time, place,
unfold from there. And sometimes, the Main
surprisingly project what is coming in the narr
Howard's brilliant and bold Main Title music
my favorite Main Title sequences ever. Befor
hearing what is to come … And whatever it is,
than we can imagine. The Main Titles from
counterpoint to the quiet suspense that fills t
That violent, muscular, angular, orchestral mus
first act. The audience is on the edge of their s

LINKS MENTIONED IN THIS CHAPT

My YouTube Channel
https://www.youtube.com/c/ BillBrownMusic/videos

Mallory Battle (Michael's Theme)
https://shorturl.at/pwLyP

Michael's Theme Demo - Dominion Season 2
https://soundcloud.com/ billbrownmusic/michaels- theme-original-demo

︎APTER FOUR

︎BUSINESS

︎ere preparation and opportunity meet.

︎n to be ready for those opportunities!

︎a long way in this business, but you need more
︎those, being easy-going, humble, open to new
︎ation are keys to success. As collaborators,
︎are helping those people we're collaborating
︎ass any expectations they might have about
︎and, just as importantly, enjoying the process
︎ant for your first encounters with your peers in
︎ay through your life. It's more fun to work with
︎and always excited and hardworking enough
︎be, knowing that person will give 110% every
︎to, but because they are so passionate about
︎ss for the faint of heart, but if you look at it
︎thing to be able to do for a living. To do what
︎akes it incomparable, really.
︎mend most to anyone just starting out *(or in*
︎as many directors, producers, developers,
︎possible as you travel across your unique
︎hips. To make those connections, to nurture
︎g relationships is *essential* to any composer's
︎ntern at a film company or music production
︎r, to learn about the business and make new
︎a composer's studio and learn the ropes in
︎y young composers do. Everyone's path is
︎ing!

Some resistance might occur when you
to get out there and make those connection
your career. I can totally relate! Most compo
within the confines of their studio, safe from t
… you have to stretch out of your comfort :
That's where the magic truly is.

I was very lucky to start my career in
Hollywood, back in the 90s, as it was alrea
world and connected to the television and fi
a music editorial division upstairs working o
the day, sound designers designing all the s
all the business things … and I was there ev
music. This was a very unusual circumstance
probably sounds nuts to you reading this. And
I didn't realize what an incredible gift it was t
of everything that was happening there and to
producers, developers, etc., just by going into
there! Can you imagine? Shortly after I started
Soundelux and built my first home studio. Le
Soundelux closed its doors. Something about
companies and bottom-lines and all of that
also when most of the big recording stages
and Signet Sound) closed their doors forever
transitional time for all of us in the industry. Lu
DMG are still around town, though some mov
them as often as I'd like. If I could turn back th
early years again, I would. It was a really fun ti
for granted. Each one has the potential for ma

So how does all of this relate to the busine
the more relationships you have with decisio
better your chance is to 'find' work. It happens
know you and trust you. Let me break it down.
and continued to stay in touch afterwards. I
years (interning is proactive in regard to putting
helpful). One of my roommates from Berklee v
to stay with him during my first trip to Los Ange
introduced me to his boss at a production cor
happened that my working knowledge of one
sequencers (and my upbeat and sparkling pers
same week cutting sound effects for *Xena Pri*
Adventures of Hercules, and more. I was so e

nds. It was never dull! I was continually learning
 pushed me to grow by working on the dub
for projects, which allowed me to meet more
bout the filmmaking process as I went. Then I
oommate about this new division at Soundelux
vriting music for triple-A video game titles, and
ught of writing game music up until that time!
ner – I'm SO glad we met and roomed together
enerosity! You rock!)

s it unfolded in front of me without judging it
ad. I loved my little one-bedroom apartment
rk and friends. It wasn't all easy all the time,
oment, trusting that my next steps would lead
hought at the time that I would of course be
dio films anytime now, and I worked with that
re mentally, scoring the projects I worked on
had in me.

from that perspective worked for me. Maybe it
realize how the music I was writing then would
 never thought about fans or anything like that.
 for this is: live and create *as if* you're already
 the coolest project ever – because someday,
: of an audience of thousands who are on their
a third encore piece, 95 minutes into your live
of which …

COW

It was June of 2019. Fans from all over Europ
I had written 17 years before for a massively
game called *Lineage 2*. What an amazing n
know there would be fans all over the planet
hear the music live? It was such an incredible

After conducting for 80 minutes straight a
to life, played with so much passion and hear
to stand and turned to look at the audience be
in the hall was standing, applauding. I'd ne
it. My heart was so full in that moment. I too
could, though it was impossible to take it in fu
goodbye to all of the levels of audience befc
and exited the stage.

I'll never forget standing there with the s
now accompanied by my Russian 'entourag
I was both exhausted and exhilarated and
dressing room when Kate asked me politely
'just wait a minute'. Then I stopped and listene
and then louder with joyful noises. It continu
5 minutes (I have no idea how long it was) u
me and whispered, "Okay, go ..." My heart w
walked through the doors and the audience e
love in the room. It was, well ... Can you imag
idea. This is what is so beautiful about life.

I had three specific intentions going into t

1. To have fun
2. To really connect with the orchestra
3. To share my deep gratitude with the au

But this was so much more than I'd exp
the music and recording *Lineage 2* was a g
altogether. This was a milestone in my life. A c
was something so wonderful that I'll never eve

This might seem like it's separate from tl
but I think the energy is all connected. I wa
videos and photos that week from rehearsals,
and at the live concert, which was just a ramp
flooded with fan videos and photos from the c
most incredible experiences I've had.

The only thing standing in the way of c
sphere of influence is *you*. It starts with that

way around the world and back … to a career
or films. I had no idea that friendship would
g all of the awesome friends and colleagues
ncredible experiences I've had. But it did. And
ain, who knew, right?

ased in Los Angeles, wrote:

s often daunting and overwhelming to many
working as slowly building relationships, one

fine line between eagerness and annoyance,
ne to learn where that line is." I encourage
ollow up, to be outgoing and friendly. But also
omething go, and move on.
od listening skills and please do not interrupt
d maintain good eye contact.
re reaching out to someone, be informed.
they have written, recent lectures, industry
ts. Take a little time to come prepared before

ne for "10 minutes of their time" is something
to find out practical advice. I've always been
nal growth, at all stages of my career. I find that
vice. Ask for the best career advice they were
at NOT to do as you continue to expand your
nd brand. And stick to the 10 minutes! Everyone
ne. And always send a thank you note!
to meet many key industry executives and
ne involved in groups and organizations that
into college extension classes, lecture series,

ased in Nashville, wrote:

kers will want to meet you when you have a
an artist, an opportunity). They are less likely to
because you want to get to know them. Those
e by close friends of the decision-maker and
oductive. A decision-maker is in the business of
n a 'yes' piece of business and you're in.

GETTING THE PROJECT

"I find that the harder I work, the more luck
Jefferson

"All progress takes place outside the com
Bobak

"Success seems to be connected with actic
moving. They make mistakes, but they don"

This business is like riding waves. You catch a
It can be exhilarating, challenging, fun, and ho
riding it. Then the wave crashes on the sand a
to ride again, you can swim out through a bu
that awesome ride again. The metaphorical 'w
refer to how difficult it is to find the next gi
(mentally) to tread water and wait. What I ca
that there *is* another wave out there. It might
it might feel like it's never going to happen,
fun you've ever had when you find it. I've ha
already. With hard work, patience, and persev

I believe that 'grit' (i.e., perseverance/d
towards your goals) is one of the most importa
Along with that, you'll need the self-awareness
about what your business is, what its value is,
to how you show up in the world. Director C
director: Mission Impossible: Fallout/Jack Re
thinking about the business as something you
of yourself as a business to be acquired. Your
demonstrate your value. Ask yourself if the lott

Wherever you're starting from, whether it's
the next job at some point down the line in yo
to learn new skills, keep creating, and take yc
Demonstrate your value either on your curre
showcasing your vision, technical skill, and ur
the scenes/making-of video on social media
more about your personality and could spark
newest work on social media, or direct mes
with in the past and have relationships with,
everyone up to date. And remember that bri

nt; getting together for coffee, lunch, dinner,
' it happens to be. That's where you'll really
ships. The good news is there is more content
r, and you are in control of how you can create
that will allow you to score that content.

ESS PLAN?

out or 'starting over' in this business, you're
starting out, one way to 'create, improve, and
intern or assist for a composer or composing
comparable position would be the PA on a film
d runners who went on to become directors,
nd more. The same can be said of many
terns over the years who climbed to the A-list
s. The more skills you come into the workplace
ill be to them and the better your chances of
iough my first internship in NYC was unpaid
s, basically), I still was able to learn more than
ology, studios, and the business. Along with
tudio (I helped build it during my time there)
demo and album material. I didn't get my first
at experience, but it was a step in the right
et! While I was doing that, I worked at a music
v months, still writing and recording for myself
time to move on though … Los Angeles was
d composing for a living was my destiny (play
Ark theme here).
nposer who is 'in-between successes' or is
sn't know where the next one is coming from?
tainty, it becomes fear; **when we accept it, it**
are always opportunities around every corner,
whether they're something we didn't expect at
next opportunity is about to come knocking?
and excitement, we might have some insight
ike to take action.

TIPS ON GETTING THE NEXT SCOR

1. Be Proactive

The other day, I received a brief from a f
composer. It was sent to a large list of peo
looking for recommendations. I emailed back,
offered to score a few scenes for their film.
feature films, which were due to start in a fev
tried out some things that were a bit different a
took a few hours, but I had tons of fun and had
looked like. The producers replied saying the
them – even citing specific spots in the music
that they would keep this in mind as they cor
Just be proactive!

2. Be Grateful

I thanked the producer profusely for the oppor
we can work in this field (and make a good, de
eternally grateful for that.

SHOULD I TAKE THIS GIG? WHAT S

Fee: $10k – $50k

I told a friend that he could absolutely quote h
wanted him to know that prospective agents
with a bigger resume than his, who would ta
work. In the end, I told him to quote an amc
about, because, as we all know, *it's going to b*

Keep in mind, there are other creative way
the box. For example, I've heard of composer:
their services, along with a license fee for th
retain the rights to the music and are being
creative fee for their time spent working on the

Ownership Rights

I told my friend that if it he would be working
was not in the business of monetizing its m
on keeping the rights to his publishing and m
media/WW/In Perp **license** to the music he cr
inhibit film distribution *at all*.

I didn't talk to him about this, but if he
a lot of various deal points that needed to

npany's publishing entity might receive (sync
, mechanicals, streaming, digital sales, sheet
10se issues may be enough to scare an indie
:n wanting the WFH language.
ne to you that is simply a no-brainer in regard
or pass. You know the director or team is great
1spiring and challenging in the best possible
Ve all love those jobs, right? But with budgets
industry shifts, competition widening, and
ome more accessible to everyone, sometimes
is is when you need to take a step back and
own personal and business perspective.

t bring to you/your business?
excited about?

king opportunities?
create something new/fresh? (The chance to
n?)
great people, enjoying the process of

siness bring to the project?
ed relationship within the project? (Trust is so
s. If we already have that trust with a director
sets, we're on our way to getting that gig!)
int of view on the project/score?
I set that no one else can offer?
eally confident and excited about? If so,
(Have you written music that fits the project
o write new demo music to get the gig?)
rd similar ideas on how to get your next (or
shared the same advice myself as a mentor

iel Ciurlizza, outlined the process clearly in an
ammates.
t me share it here (on the following pages).[1]

dapted for this book.

HOW TO GET SCORING PROJEC⌐
(AND CONNECT WITH FILMMAK

(See Link to this article on page 76).

1. LOOK FOR GIGS (FROM ANYWHERE ▶
Try finding filmmakers on sites like Vir.
noticed that the production quality there
higher than other places. You could also
Reddit, IndieGoGo, Facebook, or anywhe
their content.

- **REDDIT** - Looking through r/filmmakin⟨
  gamedev, or r/gameDevClassifieds wou
  start when looking for filmmakers or ga⟨
  work you enjoy. It's important to offer v
  communities (rather than pitching every
  time engaging with and learning about
  before pitching.

- **FACEBOOK** - Going through Faceboo⊦
  filmmaking might yield great results. Th⟨
  looking to share insightful content, and
  recent award winners or films they've p⟨
      While following the page of Filmma⁏
  dedicated to helping upcoming filmma⊦
  posted about a film that had just won a
  up the filmmakers and loving all the wo⟨
  through these same 6 steps and we en⟨

- **INSTAGRAM** - This can be a great way
  production. If you're already following f⟨
  with, go to their profiles and follow the ⟨
  On top of that – or if you're starting fror
  like #filmmaking or #indiefilm to look fo⟨

Here are some hashtags I've assemble⟨
frequency of use (how quickly the 'Most Re⟨

#filmmaking   #filmphotooftheday
#filmmakerlife #filmmakinglife #filmfestivals
#filmdirecting #moviestill #moviestills #

duction   #indiefilm   #independentfilms
endentfilmmaker   #independentfilmmaking
#cinematographer   #makingmovies
#featurefilms #featurefilm

Outlier IG posts to attract filmmakers, but
built relationships with fantastic teammates
ators like Roland Bingaman.
e engaged in the communities we're looking
and Reddit *before* pitching for a job. Offer
you think you need to offer – before making
e ask and just contribute ... maybe people

u've really enjoyed, look up the filmmaker
r available work. If what they're making is
Facebook or Instagram and let them know

media approach. We're not pitching, we're

to get into what you specifically like about
ling, compelling cinematography, amazing
, if you enjoyed it!

ests and talk about your philosophies on
example, I think films driven by people-
action-focused drama) are usually far more

ave to talk about work ...
d I were talking about how we both love to
t cultural backgrounds.
talking about work anyway, since cooking
ng process.

5. DON'T SPOTLIGHT YOUR MUSIC OR

The one thing I never do is talk about my mu
it from the person I'm talking to, it's just th
is more exciting for me (and generally more

Plus, there's something special about
being friendly and learning more about sc
ourselves.

6. SPOTLIGHT THEIR ACHIEVEMENTS

A really fun thing I love about our Instagram is
series (we're the only ones using that has
post about our favorite films.

It's best to do this when a filmma
premiered so we can help with its awaren
done this with year-old projects before to
the types of films we love, support and enc
work we admire, and continue building on
the community. People really appreciate the

FRIENDS LOVE WORKING WITH

Once you two get going, there's a good ch
you for your interesting ideas. Keep up
working on and continue being a genuine fa

In time, your new friend will discover –
– that you're pretty good at writing music
see *you* succeed just as you do for them.

Ultimately, just as great people enjoy cc
– friends love working with friends.

THE PITCHING PROCESS

What This Is About
(And How You Can Use It)

This is about finding work (even without
connecting with people you want to work w

Most of the projects we've gotten
connections and word of mouth. That saic
more active approach to finding more proje

Our team has developed this pitching

long process, we've lost out on a lot of really
o landed some amazing opportunities.
ne easier-to-get projects just to consistently
f that allows us to experiment with musical
mmunity.
epending on what your goals are, but I've
cture works for just about any job – even
(which I've also tested with great results.
genuine interest.)
who we've pitched to the most – indie

strategy works for indie filmmakers and
e of the largest projects in the world. In
king for passionate people who find ways to
ten as possible.

you're looking for, you can browse YouTube,
d other crowdfunding sites) for indie films
IMDb for long-form films in development.
those:

the search bar and type 'proof of concept
re, you can sort by upload date and view
search is 'short film filmmaker'.' If you're
genre, you could type 'sci-fi' or 'drama'
es.

'Staff Picks' or 'Categories' sections. Staff
a lot of traffic coming to the filmmakers,
little harder than ones that haven't gotten
g through categories will bring up different
e exploring their 'Narrative' section.

eck out their 'Film' section and look for
nd new or almost funded. Some of these
nded, but I think the priority should be the
ell, if you like the project enough, shoot
've made connections that way, too. If

you're not in a position to take that c
will definitely get funding.

- **INDIEGOGO** - Same as Kickstarter.
  section and peruse!

- **MOVIE INSIDER** - You can search b
  like going for projects in developmen
  on the team behind a project likely w
  experience. Searching for them on IM
  Google search might help.

- **IMDB PRO** - You can search what p
  working on here. I like going into the
  Netflix or Amazon Studios) to see wh
  production.

2. Pick Something You Connect With

Pick a project you really connect with and
you can on the story. Figure out what it's a
there's a book, read it or get the cliff notes
who the director, writers, or producers are.

3. Create A Short Custom Demo Based (

If you have access to any of the project's n
a demo of what you think the music should
between 2 to 3 minutes long and cover a
might hear in the movie we're pitching for.
content that matters, especially if they'll be
they likely will.

This action – taking the time to write
shows your work ethic and investment in the
sending them a demo before they're expe
in more work than they were ever expecting
already on the project).

Most composers will come in asking if th
come in, wasting no time, already having a p
More often than not, you're going to ge

kage

dios site to host your pitch or, if you prefer,
mble your pitch.

director explaining how much you enjoy the

look like (*Template last updated Oct. 22,*

ir name], how can I contribute? [or "Love
I help?"]

pany Name] Team),

d I recently saw/heard/read about your film,
[platform/person] and really enjoyed the
cularly [key element you enjoyed]. Offering
the industry(via story and film) is something

the world of [FILM TITLE] that I wrote music
you can find that here (along with my vision

love to expand on these ideas and talk with
to the project!

ploring this further, [Filmmaker]!

omposer

mber]

you do, consider using software like Yesware
people are opening your emails. It can also
follow up with them after we've pitched.
spond right away – they're either too early in
get. That follow-up software will help with this.
ek. Then maybe two weeks after that. I play
what kind of project it is. Many projects have

longer development/pre-production period
so they may not be ready to think about mu

6. Nurture The Relationship
You might get the project you pitched for ...

Ultimately, you've made a connecti
creativity you admire (and you've made a gre
were at it). If you sustain this relationship b
and generous, good things can happen.
recommended by someone that 'you've nev

Plus, the more you support our fellow
community around us becomes.

7. How Can This Process Improve?
I can't promise that this is the best process
is based on your personal style. But I think
building a relationship from scratch.

That said, if anyone has additional th
know them. Can you think of ways this prc
sort of effective pitching techniques do you

Check out Daniel's site for lots of rea
awesome. (See Link on page 76).

ON CREATING DEMOS

I thought it might be helpful to share what I've
demos for potential clients and projects. I don
rules for this, but this is what I've learned any
will be useful to you. Here's a list of some thin

Keep your demo to 10 tracks or less. If you
great. If you're adding tracks just to fill space

1. Tailor your demo to the client/project.
   sending the demo to and, more import
   specifically what they are looking for an
   that vein, or write some new things tha
   instrumentation.

2. If you don't have a musical direction bu
   send a demo anyway, try to have it refl
   composer. You don't have to do everyt
   best and share the kind of music you lo

elf within the 10 tracks. Remember that
obably has a limited amount of time to listen,
ur best tracks first. If they hear five cues in a
ne, they'll probably zone out and lose interest.
ing while maintaining #2 and #3.

in your tracks; surprise your listeners in a
ssible. Unexpected harmony, rhythms, sound
n. Try to think outside the box. And keep it
ements as the piece progresses.

The more intimate the recording of the live

ReelCrafter for sending demos and cataloging
ed great! Check it out.
za suggests including images that accurately
tching for.

AKER USING YOUR DEMOS

time to check this out! Here are some of the
etch for [Film Name Here]:
ok at [this film's character] and his/her

hilarating, dangerous, and dramatic.
also heart. They do it for reasons important

ing goes well for our character, so we need
gh these situations.
important part is that the audience has a
m with a story that really hits.
e emotion of the story in very broad strokes.
expand on themes and vibes as the story

e' instead of 'I' here. This is a great way to
ucer/developer that you are excited about

It may be good to include a picture of yourself somewhere on the pitch so that people can:

1. See your award-winning smile
2. Say to themselves, "I want to work with this person. They look confident, relaxed, and fun!"

CONTACT
Your Name
Film Composer | [Your Business Name]
[Your Phone No.] | [Your Email]
Representation: (if applicable)
[Agent Name]
[Agent Contact Info]

LINKS MENTIONED IN THIS CHAPT

How To Get Scoring Projects (And Connect With Filmmakers)
https://www.outlierstudios.co/intres/connectwithfilmmakers

Daniel Ciurlizza
https://www.danielciurlizza.com/

HAPTER FIVE

E AGENT/
AGER MYTH

─────

o prepare for tomorrow is to concentrate
ll your enthusiasm, on doing today's work
only possible way you can prepare for the
How to Stop Worrying and Start Living

ere because I've been there, with and without
er. If you're thinking, "If I just had a great agent,
, or big triple-A game titles, or the coolest new
I used to … *Stop!* Unfortunately, most often,
truth is, you have to make it happen yourself
can help you take it further. You make it happen
makers, getting the gigs, working super hard,
ving more than you've promised every time, on
one your craft, and pour your soul into the work
ourney you find yourself writing the music for a
can't expect someone to do all of that for you.
ergy and momentum of our careers. It's about
te and the work we do when those friendships
ation. And then, when you're ready, when your
nentum, management can help you with the
u can continue to concentrate on the creative
s. That is what great management does with
uper helpful when you're busy on all of those
ds you've made!
reer is really firing on all pistons and the projects
ed some notoriety, your agent or manager can

77

also help find or make connections for you th
energy they need to do that comes from th
created. And that continues that way througho
having an agent will find you work and 'make yc
even if you sign with an agent before your care
likely spend your time 'wishing' for things to h
a lot more fun pouring yourself 100% into new
possible to create in the moment. The possibilit

To sum it up, representation usually follow
found success. I didn't have an agent until I
NY for almost a year. Working on that show gc
called me. The advice I would give you is t
producers/developers, etc., who are in a simila
and offer to help them. CSI: NY came to me
eight-year process that started with doing a
('spec ad' is a term that comes from the a
known as a spec commercial and is specula
advertisement). He loved what I did, hired me t
then called me a couple years later to meet
their new spinoff. After that series ended, that
to the creator of Dominion, and on it goes.

That same idea needs to be mirrored in o
time and nurtured in order to create a lasting
with a lot of 'buzz', the phone won't ring by its
it happen myself. Management essentially tak
of things so I can focus on the creative side
The next gig usually comes from a previous re
Sometimes, an agent can make an introductio
is not the norm. If you score a really succes
buzz, then the calls start to pour in, and that's
like hitting the jackpot, especially now, with ter
vying for the same jobs, compared to ju
competing for jobs 20 years ago!

Cold-calling or cold-emailing productions c
favor if you are able to make a real connection.
to find out more about the person or productio
you might have in common with them, or with t
if that would be a meaningful enough reason
connect. Don't try to 'sell' yourself, but instead
about the project and the person and remembe

petition and say you're going to do it better.
competition and say you're going to do it

faster; Collaboration makes us better." –

tions could be equally as powerful. We are at
sten with the intention of really hearing what
sed to just listening to answer. That's very
t the most powerful way to find new work is
e who know and trust you. That is simply the
it usually comes from referrals, unless you are
roject that is a hit with lots of industry buzz. So
friendships early on and knocking their socks
easy-going, fun, helpful, knowledgeable, and
s so important.
osers is another way young composers can
even begin working on projects, sometimes
taking over projects for their mentors. Earlier in
ants start their careers, and I've heard of many
omposer teams.
ough to work on a project that has a lot of buzz
ne will start to ring all by itself. That's the nature
e a lot to do with having a manager; managers
get that big project, which is also the nature
with a show as big as *CSI: NY*, it didn't have a
urrounded by so many similar shows (including
e). It didn't stand out in the eyes of the industry,
ff the hook like it did when I was doing triple-A
ne power of a hit project that resonates with
but the power of building relationships in the
equally powerful. Remember that!
it can be helpful to have an agent or manager
our career is ready for it) is that they can have
, scheduling, and anything that comes up as
nt, helping you navigate the business side of
to focus on the positive, creative side of your
r and team. The clearer you are with your
r it will be throughout the project. How and

79

when your fee will be paid also depends on
time in your contract. The standard method i
three payments, depending on the length of
the payment is usually made as you begin th
created in the contract for the next and final pa

A general 'indie' composing contract m
following (this is also an example of helping so
intention of building a relationship).

November 5

TO:

FROM:

RE: Bill Brown, compo

Dear Director Friend of mine,

The following will set forth the basic ter
between you, my awesome director frien
Music, Inc. F/S/O Bill Brown ('Composer')
and license the musical score ('Score') fo
known as 'Cool Movie' ('Picture'):

1. **Services:** To compose, orchestrate,
    the score for the picture, which migh
    per our discussion.

2. **License Fee:** Producer shall pay Co
    the License Fee for all composing,
    recording, performing, and packaging

3. **Deferred Fee:** Provided that (
    recognizably in the Picture, Compose
    an amount equal to **6%** of Compan
    Profits shall be defined in accordar
    hereto and incorporated herein by thi:

EXHBIT A

Net Profits shall be defined as follows:

(i)   'Gross Receipts' shall mean all sums
      exploitation of the Picture in any an
      received by Company on a non-refun

e those sums remaining from Gross Receipts

ollowing in the following order:

d/or sales agency fees paid to or deducted by

s charged by third parties and/or actually paid

ion of the Picture (which amount shall include

/or expenses associated with the financing of

premiums payable to equity investors).

fees, collection and checking costs, trade

currency conversion costs, and taxes (non

e computations, it is understood that the Net

ned in a manner that is no less favorable than

define any other cast members' share of Net

e.

o keep and maintain accurate books and

the one Picture and the proceeds derived

y agrees to provide the participant with

to the Picture once per calendar year. The

r representative shall have the right to examine,

an audit to be made of the books and records

ning only to the one Picture during regular

ich participant's sole expense. Artist shall have

ducer's books and records no more frequently

n and only with respect to statements received

o (2) years prior to the commencement of the

ment that has been issued more than two (2)

eemed incontestable).

e terms of this Agreement, Composer shall be

e owner of the Score, defined as all of its

ts underlying compositions, and retain all rights

ng but not limited to all audiovisual, soundtrack,

rmance rights, in Perpetuity.

agrees to grant an irrevocable, non-exclusive

roducer's use of the Score solely in connection

ng in- and out-of-context trailer, promotional,

n all media now known or hereafter devised,

throughout the World in Perpetuity.

Composer acknowledges that in the e
Producer's obligations under this certifica
to Composer shall not be irreparable or o
to a right to injunctive or other equitable re
that his rights and remedies in the event
be limited to the right, if any, to recover
set forth herein and in no event shall Cor
of any such breach to rescind this agreer
Producer hereunder or to seek or obtain a
including, but not limited to any relief wh
distribution or exploitation of the Picture
derivative work based thereon.

Producer agrees to provide Composer
Composer wishes to release a Soundtrac

(vi) **Expenses:** Composer shall not be re
i. Tape stock, mag stock, or any transf
   any kind.
ii. Music transfers.
i. Recording of songs.
ii. Licensing of songs.
iii. Licensing of music not composed by
iv. Music editing/music editor costs inclu
vii. Cost of live musicians beyond th
   Composer.
viii. Vocalist/Lyricist and or song expense
ix. Pre-scoring, Re-scoring, Re-recor
   reasons outside the control of the Co
x. Any and all re-use or new-use fees.

4. Screen Credit: Composer shall rec
the main titles on a separate card same
producer to read: 'Music by [YOUR NAME

5. Paid Advertising: Credit to read:
appear in all paid advertisements, includir
where Writer, Producer, and Director are
customary exclusions except that if Write
accorded credit. Composer shall also be c
size and stature of type equal to that of W

82

se file completed cue-sheets with BMI.

and correspondence to be directed to:

D:

_____

5 NAME]

_____

tract, but you will find similar language even in
ther or not the project is 'Work for Hire' (owned
or is 'licensed' is a key factor. In a situation
ence, doing the score for free, I maintained all
d to releasing a soundtrack album. Usually in
o films, the production company maintains all
poser is paid a fair creative fee for their work.
nes as a 'package fee' that includes all funds
d collaborators on the project and it is up to
at package fee as discussed with the director/
gers/agents usually take a fee somewhere in
of the package fee.
or learning more about how to find composing
cforincome.com – Check it out and say hi to
w)

THIS CHAPTER:

ne
rincome.com/

CHAPTER SI

IT'S ABO
RELATIONS

(Promotion, social media, and the se

*"You can make more friends in two months
other people than you can in two years by
interested in you." – **Dale Carnegie***

*"Talk to someone about themselves anc
– **Dale Carnegie, How to Win Friends anc***

My friend, director Joshua Caldwell was
bit about our collaboration over the yea
projects completed since we started working t
it continues to be an inspiring creative friendsh

DIRECTOR'S PERSPECTIVE:
I've worked with Bill on four feature films, i
and Infamous, two short films and a digital s
of a masterclass in creative collaboration.

My first significant interaction with E
production of Dark Prophecy, when I was
understand the depths of film scoring. Sittin
(the creator of CSI) and Bill, discussing the mu
series, was an early test of my editorial judgm
the initial theme ideas, it wasn't quite hitting
a novice, tasked with supervising and deliv
to a seasoned composer. Despite the initial
feedback, Bill's professionalism shone throug

ents in detail. It was one thing to send notes
explain them face to face. During this meeting,
hat shifted our dynamic. Bill realized that my
ning the project, not just critiquing for the sake
eraction established a foundation of mutual
, pivotal for our future projects.

nd understanding proved invaluable during
as particularly challenging due to its unique
xed light elements with serious undertones.
matched this tone was a struggle, leaving
ces for the final score. Bill and I honed the
of back and forth and conversation about the
sent over a cue that resonated with the film's
tely and the rest of the score was quickly
out our solid foundation, I doubt we could
did, and the film would have suffered from a
k. This is a testament to the enduring value
orative relationship with a composer.

just see Bill as my composer but as an
creative circle, which includes my DP and
just about working with talent; it's about
understand and amplify your vision. The
onship can be particularly challenging
ten communicate in the language of emotion
I musical terms. Bill has been instrumental
ct ideas into concrete notes, melodies, and
with him has significantly sharpened my
ghts in ways that he can creatively interpret,
nment with the film's narrative.

composer I work with; he's a cornerstone
s. Each score he crafts isn't merely music;
storytelling. What sets Bill apart is his ability
film, but to the filmmaker. That's why, for
having Bill on board isn't just preferred, it's
more than accompany the visuals; it elevates
piece of the puzzle fits perfectly into the
o weave.

r, Producer, and Screenwriter)

Promotion

In the summer of 2015, when I brought my g[...]
cello on 'Michael's Theme' for Dominion, I t[...]
process and posted it on my YouTube chann[...]
and Instagram. That first video of us recordin[...]
week on my YouTube channel and more on Fa[...]
before long. A cool fan-made video for my s[...]
wonderful character played by Carl Beukes in[...]
views. While I was scoring the show, I posted a[...]
score on my social media along with the direct[...]
cast and crew. It was so much fun getting to[...]
through all the posts, talk about the series in r[...]
an entire community of creatives. It was also[...]
connections and friendships in the industry an[...]
I was making on the series.

Deran Sarafian, Vaun Wilmott, and Bill worki[...]

Teaming up with a PR company can he[...]
audience and help promote your work. I v[...]
after finishing the season to also get the wor[...]
connected me with Variety, The Hollywood R[...]
handful of other industry outlets for interviews[...]
the music, and my process. That company als[...]
TV music and game music panels at San Di[...]
Wondercon for the next two years, which was[...]

Diego Comic Con – SDCC

ews, and the panels themselves were fun to be
n't cheap at around $50k per year, but *Dominion*
buzz on its own to get that level of exposure. And
ntent for the PR during that time after the show,
rk for me and maybe not the most productive
to new directors, showrunners, developers, and
more productive use of my time.
hiring a PR company can be invaluable is
an Emmy, Oscar, Bafta, or other award. That
te is a win-win for you and makes your chances
With an agent or manager, when it's your time,
ith PR, it has more to do with *what stand-out*
your career that they can take advantage of.

My experience was that the PR Company ha
outlets (Variety, The Hollywood Reporter, man
and if the material was current and compelling
to get articles about the work in those ma
working on a hit film or show with tons of b
opportunity for a PR team to really get you out
working on a show with a lot of buzz is that d
music, connected with that film or show, an
lead to the next jobs organically. Taking into c
drawbacks of hiring a PR company, I feel it wa

Here's an example of just a couple days
company, based on my work on season 2 of th

Morning Bill,

How are you? I followed up with SyFy again re:
along for a Twitter chat on July 30th as we di
work for you? I'd like to chat about mini-bloggi
are bad for you to talk. Are you available tomor
I can also be available to talk before or after yo

Also, in order to launch your YouTube chann
resemble your other pages so that your bran
easily identify you. A few strategic ways to do

- Use the same cover photo as on Facebook
- Cover photo dimensions are: 2560 X 1440 p
- Use the same profile photo as on Facebook
- Update the "about" section. I would recom
  your bio: Bill Brown is an award-winning c
  behind the musical scores of fan-favorite
  thrillers, dramas and super-hero adventure
  experimental approach to developing a un
  dynamic orchestral landscapes, Bill is bes
  compelling musical backdrop for all nine se
  CSI: NY. His music will soon be heard on
  apocalyptic thriller, Dominion.
- Add your website, Facebook, Twitter and S
  "About" section
- Here is a YouTube video on how to a
  YouTube https://youtu.be/o4VJCDAHq-s

Here are a few more post ideas for this we
Dominion UK premiere is today at 1PM PST.

is tweet: https://twitter.com/colinandjo1/
784

if you're ready for the premiere of #Dominion

hell breaks loose for #Dominion premiere! @

e5 of #Dominion with @VaunWilmott, @
ntire crew! [Attach photo just prior to spotting
e photo]

exclusive cue clips from #Dominion premiere
yUK http://ow.ly/PE3yS

I received from @GoSeeTalk! Check out the
w.ly/PCSuM#composer #Dominion

ething's about to bury David Whele, he hits a
Composer @AnthonySHead [Attach photo_

ue to rise in this week's episode of #Dominion?
ast week on @SoundCloud! http://ow.ly/PCThb

ninion premiere at #ComicCon last week. RT If
k! #SDCC2015 [Attach a photo from Dominion

e again this week? Listen to these cues for
ow what you think! http://ow.ly/PCV0m

scene had your favorite #cue tonight? RT for a
ive clip released on @SoundCloud. #Dominion

. #Music #Quote [Attach photo_Quote_Music

#exclusive #Dominion #cue so far?
PE3yS

s videos of my #composing process for
Tube channel! http://ow.ly/PE4eY

music in @DominionSyFy so far! I've been
gInc synths! [Attach Moog_Synths]

if you're #Theme Michael. FAV if
Hear them both on @Soundcloud. @
y/PCTEd **To post after you Gabriel's theme

Facebook

- WEDNESDAY: I don't give any #spoilers ir
  but I won't deny that the story in @Domin
  more in this article and let me know what
  to. http://ow.ly/PCSMy

- THURSDAY: Will the Angel Army continue
  #Dominion? Catch up with cues from last we
  ow.ly/PCThb

- FRIDAY: @Dominion fans, what scene had
  Comment below for a chance to have an e
  SoundCloud!

- MONDAY: Catch behind-the-scenes vide
  Dominion scores on my @YouTube channel

- IG

- Did you see the great interview @Go
  DominionSyFy composer @BillBrownMusic

- So cool! @MoogInc, @DominionSyFy, Rea
  composer @BillBrownMusic in this @Go
  PCSMy

- In preparation for the next episode of @Do
  to #MichaelsTheme by @BillBrownMusic. In

- What will we hear next from @BillBrownM
  #Dominion...

- What is the difference #composing for #ga
  BillBrownMusic had to say in this @GooSe
  PCSMy

Hi Bill,

We're going to send you our updates separatel
We finally heard back from SyFy and it seems
strategy ideas that we had, however they are i
to retweet your content, and also reiterated th
you participate in the live TW Q&As and Face
provide them questions for them to moderate a

Since SyFy won't be leveraging the ideas that
move forward with that on our own. Each wee
want to upload cues to SoundCloud to promote
like to share a Dropbox account of cues with
following each episode?

This means our strategy for Dominion includes

stions that SyFy moderates with.

n retweet your content.

process.

end on social with your cues after they air.

ndCloud cues.

for our Comic Con panel! See attached. A few
ontent.

for next week:

omicCon? I'm stoked to be participating on
Fy Thrills & Chills panel. You can catch me
eSieur, and @ChrisRidenhour on July 10th at
we talk about how we evoke your goosebumps
[Attach panel]

…[Attach Dominion countdown graphic]

x Let me know whose theme you think you will
s #Dominion [attach image 1]

n me at the @SYFYTV #BehindtheMusic panel
idenhour on 7/10! [Attach poster]

doing in 10 days? #Dominion #DominionS2

watching the premiere of #Dominion from
ced #Dominion panel http://bit.ly/1LotPAh

and #composertips on how to #score intense
Music [Attach poster]

horrorconnoisseur, then this interview with @
sert link]***when the interview is released.

#SDCC #BehindtheMusic panel with @
n S2!

s #Moog synths, is composing for #Dominion
ur #BehindtheMusic panel on 7/10 at #SDCC.

yTV's hit-show #Dominion S2 @BillBrownMusic
Music Thrills & Chills panel on 7/10.

HOW TO USE SOCIAL MEDIA EFFE

Social media is not truly what moves your c
and friendships in the industry really move it
conversations work better in person. Tone
expressions need to be seen, and energy felt. V
the de-facto norm since the pandemic lock-c
solely via zoom, but nothing beats meeting ir
for that reason can be tricky. Learning to put
maintaining what makes you YOU is the challe
is only *one* you, and that is your power.

Using social media wisely, you can con
business connections, and nurture relationsh
portfolio of work. Making those connections, ge
of your collaborators/clients, and having those
ones will take your career to the next level. I've
and feel more connected to our community as
one of the main ways we connect and commur
use of video call software for calls or meetings
of the exception for many, but I still recommen
face IRL (in real life) before starting a project, an
It makes such a difference in relating to each otl
and, even more importantly, building friendsh
meeting in real life isn't an option, it is still tota
connection with clients if you really take the time
open-ended questions, and let them know you
is and how you will support it. Consistent com
preparation, delivering on time every time, keer
light at heart, empathic/understanding, and no
and being ready to change direction on a dim
nurturing that relationship!

We all want to feel seen, understood, cc
to serve by sharing our gifts, be appreciated,
purpose in life. Nurturing these relationships ar
rewarding in all these ways, even if it is via a vic
about how you are helping, what you are creati
with, and how you're showing up for yourself a

While I was 'in-between' successes aft
canceled, I decided to create an album of n
was called *DREAMSTATE* and was a comb
modular synths and acoustic/orchestral com

orchestra for his album Dreamstate…
.dreamstateproject.com

hare a little bit more about the making of the
www.dreamstateproject.com, which includes
of, and behind the scenes photos from the
planation of how the album was conceived.
all of it, and the album was a really healing
y after Dominion being canceled.

ia/Promotion

on social media. Remember that most times
ia 'persona' and their real life one. Take what
f salt, because there is so much more going on
the internet. Social media can be a tool we can
nd take the feedback online for what it is: just
ng a guitar up to an amp and turning it up …
od, some bad. It's how you use it that matters.
ne says to you is just a reflection of where they
ess (how they feel about themselves or where
motionally in that moment). That said, here are
ocial media effectively:

uld give others insight into who you are as a
our business and career at the same time. Be
, interesting, and positive.

to followers. Share your behind the scenes in
insightful way.

er ad' for yourself or brag.

eact to events/films/shows/artists, post
ive insights, etc., and add hashtags! (#SXSW,

eagues you want to connect with for what they
d hashtags) in insightful ways.

- Just like with agents, PR will come to you
  force it. In the meantime, your time might
  on creating new relationships within the in

Across your social media and website,
consistent and focused. If you compose musi
getting started), your socials and website shou
while expressing what makes you unique. V
industry being your target audience, you wa
unique, great at what you do, fun to work with,
that you and your time are valuable.

Doing professional photo shoots and hav
photographers at your live events or recordir
idea, *it is what is expected from professionals.*
equipment for your blog or studio behind the s
of you and your colleagues/clients engaged a
great places to start. If you're just getting s
approach your promotion 'as if' you are
already there, doing what you want to do.
And keep in mind, directors and producers
have really full schedules if they are working
and will only take a moment to check out
your site, unless you are recommended by
a colleague/mutual friend. (Most often, that
is where your work will come from.)

Keep it as real and simple as possible.
You want to be honest with yourself about
where you are in your process and not
falsely 'building-up' your story either. Pros
will see that coming a mile away. And, like I
said earlier, don't forget to have fun!

LINKS MENTIONED IN THIS CHAPT

Dreamstate
*https://www.
dreamstateproject.com/*

APTER SEVEN

NG BALANCE
H TEAMWORK

ar belief, you don't have to do it all

ibedded in my subconscious that the best film
t all themselves. I believed deep down that their
ible musical footprint was specifically and only
not true, though. Even John Williams has had
)rchestrators, arrangers, score and parts-prep
musicians, seasoned scoring engineers, dub
itive process itself are crucial to his process.
ive those incredible scores without all of that
ie? It's a relief to know that John Williams and
's that have come before us and paved the way
ime point in the process of creating, they had

ive discovered that collaboration and teamwork
ide composing so meaningful and fulfilling and
ict better than I could ever make it by myself.
recording sessions, late nights working with
cers, orchestrators, music editors, assistants,
dtracks and delivering scores, all collaborating
e are truly some of the best memories and

nas its own challenges in regard to workflow,
and of course all aspects of the business and
every project. And every project has its own
surprise versions of all of these as well. When I
< in 2004, it was the first time I had ever scored

a series of any kind, and luckily, I was paired u
music editor, Josh Winget, that had been wor
a bit. He and I became fast friends and tackle
around 26 episodes per season to the dub sta
together (breaking during the summer each y
a show runner, post supervisor, editor, music
producer or director for the spotting sessions
where music was needed in each episode. I
would take notes and then later that day create
references, notes, and cue titles and send it to
be starting to write new music for the episc
design palette and writing themes.

I'd get locked picture from editorial usuall
continue writing and prepping for some live s
and writing for a few days, my assistant wou
and creating stems of all of the cues when I fir
around was usually less than a week for each
mixes and stems to Josh as he would be prepr
the dub stage. As I was completing the score a
on the dub stage as they were dubbing/mixing
its audio elements. Then we would meet up ac
and everyone would help make sure all of th
needed them to be and were working as intenc

each episode every week was exciting. I would
s from the post supervisor or show runner, so
eady be a home run at the mix. It didn't always
have to run back to the studio and create an
e for an area that didn't have music. That was
nes nerve-wracking.
I had written something during the week that I
rned out to be perfect for that one scene that
had to tweak and mix it so I could get it back
to finish and deliver to the network that same
ould adjust things on the stage during the mix
he post supervisor or show runner wanted an
key part of what a music editor does, and it
cian/editor to do it!) Then, with that episode
he following day to spot the next episode, and
vould have an extra week in our schedule by
uld get ahead of things and would start writing
of the coming episode's picture. Any extra time
nat show was really an incredible experience.
ylistically and gave me endless opportunities
laborate with so many talented people along
ne it by myself; I don't think anyone could! It
n the production and music teams and with my

assistants over the years, with the post-produ
I miss those days, even if they were long days
breaks. It was all creatively so satisfying in th
learning/growing experience throughout.

During those summers on hiatus from the
and game projects. One year, I left the seas
straight to a meeting with the director of *The*

I literally worked all summer on
that project all the way up to the
spotting session for the premiere
episode of the next season of
CSI:NY. Josh and I finished the
final day of dubbing for the film
and the next day we were at the
spotting session!

I scored a few films during the
pandemic and subsequent lock-
down, via Zoom for the most part
(including recording orchestra
and mixing remotely). The tech

Original Moti

has gotten to the point where anyone can recc
number of musicians, even though I would high
person as much as you possibly can! Those li
of my most treasured experiences in my life.

ght and you need help with cues on a project,
: least one other additional music composer
1 hiring an assistant to help with the more
stems for the final mix (a breakout of tracks of
natching the mix as a whole) and keeping the
stead of killing yourself working crazy hours,
ur team and focus on being creative. I recently
nding the Line with director Joshua Caldwell
to help flesh out some cues, and the results
1 (per minute of music) for their time, made
the film itself, and split 'cue sheet' royalties
- collaborated on. Simple! The same goes for
oject, even if only a few, or a LOT – it makes
brings more creativity and soul to the score!
rchestrator my entire career, James Sale, who
mmate at Berklee the last two years we were
ortive and has also conducted the majority of
nd even helped me with fleshing out the full
eage 2 concert). He is the definition of grace
1 an inspiration to me all these years.

arvel's *Captain America: Super Soldier* was an
nd. But the one mistake I made in budgeting
) a resource manager. The interactive/reactive
score was really complex (and totally worth it!),

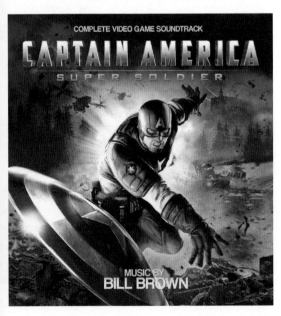

COMPLETE VIDEO GAME SOUNDTRACK

CAPTAIN AMERICA

SUPER SOLDIER

MUSIC BY
BILL BROWN

Collaboration is the key – and feedback doe

When you're at a playback meeting with
your cue playback with an excuse, explanation
they've even heard it. Directors/producers usu
about all of the technology we have to maste
much else going on, hundreds of questions a
in so many directions! The music should be th
them. Keep things chill, be confident, but als
it known you're having so much fun with this
you're totally open to ideas.

Stay engaged and excited. And stay cur
great way to approach everything in life, not
notes, really listen, to understand them. Ref
heard them say, and if no ideas spring fourth i
down and keep going.

If you have an idea in the moment based
Sometimes, that conversation leads to a greate
of what would serve the scene better, and to n

Remember, this isn't concert music or 'a
calm, confident, and light on your feet in those
part of your job. You don't have to sell yourself
listen to understand, reflect back what you he
who is easy to work with. We are artists, yes. E
media in collaboration, we are first and foremo

Carl Beukes, Vaun Wilmott, and E

SESSIONS OVER THE YEARS

ell and Bill (Infamous) See link on Page 108

Guo (Dominion Season 2 Session)

Multi-instrumentalist George Doering (Bro

*Cellist Tina Guo (Dominion
Season 2 Session)*

and Tina in the studio

Carmine Giovannzo and Tina Guo (CSI: NY/Duke Sessions)

sions)   *Peter Maunu (CSI: NY Sessions)*

Caffeine (CSI: NY Sessions)   *Steve*

My first home studio

sions)

CSI: NY Series Wrap Party at the CBS Radford Studio Lot, Los Angeles

CA

Tina Guo and Bill in the Studio (Dominion Season 2)

George Doering in the studio

Bill conducting the orchestra and recording the sta...
he composed and produced for Windows XP (Mi...

eage 2 Live' concert – 2019

NIN in the studio (Negative Film Sessions)

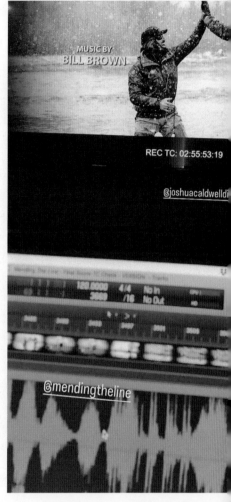

In the studio working on Mending ▸

LINKS MENTIONED IN THIS CHAPT

Captain America: Super Soldier Score

https://soundcloud.com/ billbrownmusic/sets/ captain-america-super- soldier

Bill Brown: Windows XP (score)

https://soundcloud.com/ billbrownmusic/sets/bill- brown-windows-xp-score

APTER EIGHT

AND ACTION
ROM WORKING
MPOSERS

---

and energy to those things with the most
highest return to your life" - **Me**

he lesson in everything you do in your life...
– Also me

most important things for us to gain as life is so
r all of us – all the time! I've learned through life
, which is ironic because you have to live, learn,
ective or wisdom. So I thought I'd dedicate a
e perspective/wisdom from some friends from
f you look at life as a learning opportunity, from
ience can be meaningful.
estion:

can you share in regard to creating, navigating,
s business?

The Last Samurai, The Da Vinci Code,

st often - or should I say, the question people
Question everybody really wants to know the
a career like yours?' And the honest answer is -

Maybe it's because I approached things
so much by choice - although I suppose it wa
single-minded, stubborn, and focused on one t
interest in or paying attention at school to any
Literature, Mythology, and … Music.

Music was too much a private, precious,
it ruined by the brutality of the German schoo
of kids blowing into out-of-tune Treble Recor
notes out of time on xylophones is a true test
and playing the piano in private endlessly,
complaining, was sanity and refuge from the
thrown out of eight schools for being genera
Upon coming to England, still loving music, I
A Time in the West, the Sergio Leone film, v
And that film was the great epiphany for me: I
how the magic works! You support the image
add a whole new context to your music - and
The first ten minutes of Once Upon A Time in
in the conventional sense, but Musique Con
and sound effects, brilliantly organised, a bea
sound in itself, even though it doesn't use an
made me realise that anything is music and
with courage and commitment.

I loved music but never wanted to follo
education in orchestration in the classical
listening into the music and playing, and I lea
the movies.

These were new, revolutionary times for
become somewhat affordable, and Wendy C
'Switched on Bach' synthesised sound.

The one thing I knew was going to be r
I was fascinated by synthesisers and I g
barely affordable computers and word proc
sequencers. Do any of you remember the Rolar
world's worst, yet to me most beautiful inven
It cost a fortune for a basically starving, yet d
to get really, really good at programming it to
day and night, loitering in recording studios ar
process worked, both the technology and the
perfectly average recording engineer but a re

110

ese different concepts together, because I felt
es in technology were going to play an ever
n ever before.

eally needed a mentor. I had the luck of having
oser Stanley Myers offer me a job because
complicated, yet beautiful Italian espresso
'd make coffee and in exchange I could sit in
orchestra session. I listened to Stanley, Nic
and learned from an endless stream of great
to write the little cues Stanley didn't want to
ar chases. He loathed car chases. He really
ra worked and explained to me that, without a
tarted focusing on writing tunes.

own work, mostly through the reckless trust of
(I am doing one of their films now … 40 odd
ed learning from directors like Barry Levinson,
d and got me my first Oscar nomination (I know
y European name, they thought I was probably
se composer who had paid his obscure dues
had never heard of). I also learned from Peter
chlesinger, Mike Nichols, Jim Brooks, Penney
y Scott … to name just a few - I mean, there
, I learned not just how to write a pretty piece
t how the psychology of the characters were
eenager, I was obsessed with reading Jung,
Kübler-Ross' book *On Death and Dying*. It was
ng that fascinated me; the whole Vienna school
iatrists, writers and painters, composers and
ntroversial Bruno Bettleheim, who wrote *The*
f the greatest sources you can have as a film
n on the psychology of fairytales, which to me
irror of the modern psyche and how film is the

amount of luck and recklessness plays into
ting film makers at the right time, and when I
nd with disaster and failure. You'd better have
t when the BBC fires you. When luck goes and
only one thing you can do; you recklessly say
. So when Barry Levinson rings your doorbell
offers you a Hollywood movie, you say "Yes

of course!" - even though you have no idea
psychologically prepared to hide your fear an
just enough about the human condition, from
on philosophy and too many books on psychc
museums and art books, to have the imagin
an appropriate tune that resonates and uses
in a musical context to demonstrate your
conversation with your director, right there,
yet fully orchestrated music. Which is prett
You write things which interest you as psych
human condition and you make the whole s
of discovery, of figuring it out, and use synth
a way of letting the director hear what you h
can't even imagine.

Recording the score is an interesting thi
that's being added to the film, and the musici
'actors' that are being cast. You really need tc
magnificent performance, full of life and energ
your director behind. All that was part of the
and the demo phase.

I have seen times when personality mak
technique. I had written a violin cadenza and
famously accomplished violinist and it sound
lifeless. I was convinced that my notes must
violinist played it, it had personality, fire, life, ar
it's so much about casting the right personalit

Well, what are we writing about? We are, f
and filmmakers. It is taken for granted early
write and orchestrate a melody, and that we
good and collaborate with the dubbing mixer
whole post-production crew, in fact. It's not a
about serving the film and, most importantly, it
have an experience. By the time they come
have something truthful that touches them - n
the opposite; it has to be committed and em
appropriate in helping the story. Music might
this. Within three notes, you can go from laug
do that so efficiently? You've got a powerful
write with love and respect in your heart.

(And no, I still don't know how to build a c

dal of Honor, The Boys, Lost in Space,

:

n my career early on is that I saw other aspiring

ser events and reaching out to composers for

. While assisting composers that work on much

jects is a great way to learn and hopefully pay

ips and creative partnerships come from other

enever I went to film festivals or screenings to

Coachella or Sundance with groups of music

eet and develop amazing personal friendships

collaborators to this day, I also noticed that

ser there. Go to events that feature directors,

ic supervisors above all else. And if you're just

with their assistants!

perspective of being a storytelling partner

er first:

ent dictate form." Whether that means a scene

e or a 2 note repeating bass motif or a pad for

the character need to tell his or her story in the

? Like all of us, I came out of school, wanting

writing things that drew a lot of attention. The

ects I do, the more I keep reminding myself to

nt. I try to always ask questions about drama,

d feelings … almost never about sound or

ne later. Your director wants to know how you

n touch the audience and make the audience

ly. That's it. That's the job in its entirety.

ney in yourself and your presentation:

tor or studio already has a relationship with a

o they hope to work with, or a strong (and very

mmendations from trusted advisors (producers,

ances of landing that opportunity with no real

dit list is minimal, but to expect someone to take

ed composer without providing them with a very

swer' to their need is ridiculous. If there is a job

n the vaguest connection or way to get your work

do SO MUCH RESEARCH! Google and social

se has the director done? Are there interviews

113

for the role? Past projects? Is the work based
a unique setting or genre? Do any of the decis
match yours? Did they go to the same school?
intern for someone else you admire? Do they lik
can create even the most tenuous thread of sp
also show your enthusiasm and work ethic). Us
presentation) that can make them say, "Well,
but wow, they've nailed this sound that I didn
they must really want this opportunity." I creat
hired someone to create graphics and a menu
mini arcade style enclosures to present my de
directors and every producer on the first Wreck
the film of course … but a producer took note a
and the execs at that studio still talk about it (a
Take risks! Go for it!

4. Be honest about your strengths and wea
as opportunities to grow and learn:

When the director of *Horrible Bosses* said he w
a mix of Beastie Boys, Black Keys, and Beck,
a huge fan of all three, but also that I wasn't a
person to nail the guitar sound … so I tracke
Beasties, the drummer from Beck, the guitaris
and begged them to play on the score and told
were in the studio making one of their record
and fought for album credits to make it happen
at every session, even asking them to 'guide u
possible. It was one of the best experiences e
even 10 years later, I work with the director an
time. I always admit what I don't know and I
creative partners in and on the process.

Geoff Zanelli (Pirates of the Caribbean: De
the West, The Odd Life of Timothy Green, Di

When it comes to agents, there are so many m
agencies but only one good match. They we
always good for me. My thoughts, in no particu

• Seeking an agent got me signed twice bu
  hoped. An agent seeking me led to somet

114

cured projects for me, or demo opportunities,
e connections, etc. But this was the case for
' projects. The rest come from my effort.

negotiating on my own behalf casts me in a
ike, where having an agent do it changes how
a creative vs. businessperson. Plus, I figure if
egotiation, I would just become an agent. The
d ones, anyhow!

d create an aura of professionalism. Whether
up for discussion. But remember, we are in the

ategizing overall career stuff. I play an active
ave plenty of conversations about why I should
rojects. If they suggest things I'm not interested
. I'm still driving the bus.

od for you is the one who wants you in the first
one who will sign you!

t breaking talent, some are good at sustaining
m once you've already broken in. The 'big'
etter at the latter.

gotiating that doesn't get talked about enough:
otiate a better deal on their own and don't
ned the client off, just a little, enough to create
e else to swoop in on the next job. They may
ust file it in their brain for later reference. I know
nave that story where they get a $1,000 offer,
the job well, then lose the client to someone
ey went from 'being underpaid to write music'
but now with a client who views them as a
tist second'. That's winning the battle, losing
t I mean. An agent is a buffer, and they play
gotiator so you can focus your energy where it

a recording artist having a record deal. There
are horror stories, and you don't need one on
do, if you're Taylor Swift, in which case they will

n't get talked about enough: whenever I do a
ers, someone asks, 'How do I get an agent?' I

answer with 'Why do you think you need
'Wait for them to come to you if you car
Those are both, of course, me talking to
benefited from hearing them, especially th

**Neal Acree (StarCraft II, World of Warcr
Stargate SG-1, Stargate Atlantis, Witchblac**

I have always seen my career as a chess gar
steps ahead, make smart, calculated moves,
the long haul. Here are some more specific thc

1. Make Money While You Sleep

I still make a decent chunk of my income from
I did very early in my career. Getting royalties
is generated independently of your day-to-da
when you sleep. These opportunities can be c
libraries and all the streaming content out there
than ever. Passive income like this is essentia
sporadic contract work.

2. Repeat Customers

Naturally, to build a career as an independent,
There are no guarantees in the freelance w
are essential. The best way to maintain thes
consistently high-quality work, be impeccably
part of your client's day when it comes to your

3. Reinvent Yourself

Always be prepared to change your stra
opportunities. Go where the work takes you. I s
an unexpected door opened into games, I walk
opportunity to try something new. A year later,
budget film world where I had been working a
Canada. But I never closed any doors. Over the
film and TV projects and continued to add to th

4. Invest in Your Future

Whether it means putting some of your inc
sample libraries, or hiring musicians out of p
that have potential to showcase your work, inv
in your future. This can be a scary prospec
worrying about keeping the roof over your head
a reputation for high-quality work.

t hasn't already been said, but it is essential,
of your career, to be open opportunities just
you off the ground. The closer you can stay to
but staying afloat is the most important thing.
orked as a music editor, copyist, orchestrator,
arian, and eventually cartage (setting up and
at studios). The last of which felt the furthest
g but introduced me to the people who helped

gic the Gathering: Duel of the Planeswalkers, of the Ring)

ey while you sleep' was the motto/joke among
when we'd hang out together in the beginnings
ys been in our minds, to look for opportunities
orking. Diversity again is a big one, but I'd like
olks have talked about the usual methods for
cts, orchestration, music prep, performance
c, et al). I recommend looking outside the box.
as you'd like or you feel like you're not making
enerate something new. Make an album. Start a
e disruptive.

Surrogates, Hattrick)

espect who were extremely successful. These
sional life more than once:

can eat caviar forever." The self-discipline of
mething I think most people are not willing to
skill to develop and nurture in all areas of life.

ir economy." My very first lawyer said this to me
about a production company who was taking its
dy's problem but yours that you aren't organized
e money for rent or that you are sick today or that
t nice to you. You can choose to respond to these
ude and where you decide to allocate positive or
'assignable'. But you have to be the one to do it.
because nobody is in your shoes, and, therefore,
heir radar and won't be their priority.

Tom Salta *(Ghost Recon: Advanced Warf*
Spartan Assault)

I'm a big subscriber to taking responsibility fo
owes you anything. Blaming yourself for your o
mindset because it tells you that you have the

Diversification and throwing a wide net wa
advertising, thinking it was 'beneath me', and r
my income writing music for ad spots.

Ads, film, TV, libraries, video games – co
income to keep going.

Matt Kenyon *(Composer Code podcast)*

After talking to many wise composers on
the simplest explanation is to do good work
continue building relationships and adding '
those relationships.

In terms of the financial piece, multiple
must, especially early on. You have no idea
gig is gonna come along, so a lot of my friends
stuff are supplemented by things like music pa
or Unreal Marketplace, writing music for audi
various media, streaming revenue, maybe tea
and selling some form of coaching or consult
product like a course.

If you have a family, it seems like the 'run
time is best: you build yourself a runway of in
expenses. That way, you know you can surviv
long) without going back to your day job. You
maintaining healthy self-care habits) during t
from part-time to full.

In terms of time management stuff, man, it'
tight calendar, prioritizing your days, utilizing t
method and deep work. Organizing all your
like Asana or Trello. I know this is a huge to
and balanced human being! Meditation, p
connections with people you care about it, e>
big holistic effort.

Anyway, this is my stream-of-consciousn
I've learned from the wise folks on my show.

Solid V: The Phantom Pain, Call of Duty:
ator Genisys)

self is important. If I don't have commissioned
library; if it's too soon since the last sample
sic. All the while, I have my YouTube to practice
to date with what I am up too. Basically, always
er it be from yourself or a client. There is always

eens, Black Lightning, The Neighborhood,
ouder, The Game, American Soul, Girlfriends,

wavering, relentless work ethic will be needed.
d. Your family will be needed. Your tears will
game will be needed. Your understanding will
ess will be needed. Your fearlessness will be
be needed. Your joy will be needed. Your life
You and all your mixed up, sometimes crazy
hash of thoughts will be needed. You with the
ur imperfections, will be needed. Because you
e Matrix...You have to know that you can do this!

Persia: The Forgotten Sands, Transformers:
eenage Mutant Ninja Turtles: Out of the
Game)

' personal, individual journey to discover the
There is no one-size-fits-all approach … but I

ys had MULTIPLE income streams - composing
ons of libraries. Orchestration for film, games,
es check has kept the wolf at bay for years,

come streams, I have received sage advice to
:

e music I can (well, this took only 20 years to
I somewhat assured).

ul friendships and cultivate a community of
iness of people opening doors for the talent
There is no 'vacancies list' and there is no

'job interview'. You must be wanted (as in
you are not wanted by the decision-maker
attend parties or give out business cards,
jobs. But to be wanted, you need to let all
your music, and you need to get them to li
have great food, invite everyone, give then
they will listen to it.) Every single meaningf
big time or has propelled my career forwa
friend's referral.

3. Maintain your health, both your physical a
    stamina, don't pull all-nighters; they are de
    attitude, develop an ability to cope with do
    rejection, and always look for the silver lini
    absolute desperation. Choose to be on yo
    dire situations.

Michelle Sudduth *(ChangeMakers: The Glo Leylines, Divorce Ranch audio drama)*

Before getting into specifics, I'd like to first r
composing for media, or with aspirations to b
of us to make a valuable contribution. The a
human, and being fully alive is entwined w
creatively externalize our deepest personhoo
favorite mediums, music or otherwise. All of
get hired in any creative field, and therefore, w
not a mirror, is not the deepest reflection of ou
beings. Explore and take ownership of your
after anyone invites you to share, utilize, or pur
Here are a few ideas that have shaped my fr
field of composing for media:

1. Know why you want to compose music fc
    that as the metric for deciding to take on
    to what composer peers might or might
    first projects because of money but be
    credits to get projects where the compos
    the workload.

2. Do the self-work that would enable you tc
    intelligence to your craft, not just work th

told is artistically good. Do this so that your
ou are, making it unique, raw, and, therefore, its
udied music in undergrad and through UCLA's
ıd they prepared me well for the technical skills
    But I went to graduate school and studied
ent, namely theology/ philosophy, and that has
deeper sense to write music.

no inner circle (no king or queen or kingdom in
 Don't spend time and energy trying to get into
:. There are only people making projects, some
ey are everywhere. Many of them can hire you
nd you develop a great connection, enough of
each other by making something together. I try
icipate in online forums, and have membership
oossible to meet as many people as I can. This
rations, and ultimately being recommended by
ng Academy for a film cohort through a MTv/

ead material or take classes in music theory,
your DAW, networking skills, screenwriting, and
 memoirs of people whose journey might offer
arn. I attend score study groups, have taken a
ocal and online music and business programs,
ount so I can 'read' on the go.

notionally, physically, mentally, spiritually, and
ar as you are able, you can, most importantly,
d so you can then feel up to the sometimes
 with deadlines and an array of personalities,
tem then others. I regularly talk to supportive
unch or the phone, go to yoga, and take hikes
ıood, am comfortable calling a therapist if I get
 plant-based, which has really helped me with
ıd feeling my best.

r inner connection to music, preserving and
 light inside so you can both enjoy it for all
ıally and so you can draw from it in your own
)eople. I go to concerts, hang out in orchestral
 challenge myself to play new piano pieces.

Becoming a professional artist, and espec
does not unfold in a linear way. Every working
individual story full of twists and turns that has
are today. Our authentic selves are the ones t
however, we might delay our unfolding if we try
a storyline that we think will get us to where
stepping stones that are the most suitable fit
gut, being ourselves, and taking one authentic

Tina Guo (GRAMMY Nominated Musician, C

BRAND POWER. A brand is synonymous with
encompasses your music, reputation, image
name stirs in people. I always recommend
envision who they want to be, the fully actualiz

What projects are you working on? Where
daily routine? How do you feel? What do you
can feel in your body and mind, the better. Or
who you aim to be, become that person by
would be doing.

The same applies to public persona. Soc
connection to the outside world. This is not j
but to connect with the entire human populatie
the small subsystems we each exist in.

Social media is an incredible tool that is fr
Don't think of it as 'marketing' - marketing is j
of what? Of sharing your art and your soul. In
we create music because we are passionatel
Share that fire - share what you do, what you
knows what you're creating or who you are, h
with others? How will you be 'discovered'?

There are potential artistic collaboratic
everywhere- in traditional media platforms an
limit yourself to what is already there; always th

Going back to my initial definition of 'bra
associate with you? Whether it's positive or ev
as art is subjective - some people will adore
Any type of emotional reaction is better than el
mediocre, seen as a 'copy' of another brand, c

Of course, if the majority of people dislik
something to examine there - and we can in

ve do and become as people bleeds into what
more raw or honest than our music when we

nda 4, The Boss Baby 1+2, No Time to Die,

Ranger there was a seven-minute action scene
ost four days to put together. We played it in a
hours, the entire cue was ripped to shreds. I
probably rewrote the entire cue almost eight
Js composers pour so much of ourselves into
take it personally. This is incredibly common,
en to these changes, the happier both you and

is just the beginning. Being able to improve
is equally important. While you may have a
sic will sound with live musicians (or however
is ...), not every filmmaker will understand.
chniques, learning to create and alter synths,
can make a huge difference to how your music

rewarding job. You're often huddled in a dark
urs and tight deadlines. Your music will be met
s asked to be rewritten. Embrace the process
becomes very easy to burn out in this career,
u truly love doing it.

d Creator of "Ignite Your Music Career!)

r a year of development. I was going to go the
nst it. I'd been helping thousands of musicians
up with requests. We have subscribers from
s online).

Ross Tregenza *(The Texas Chain Saw M*
Forza Horizon 5, Cyberpunk 2077, Gears of

I think discipline and committing to the amo
important. If a track has gone a bit wrong, c
it if you drill down and give it the time it need
communicative with the team you're working
on both sides of that situation, so I try to alway
what I'm doing and when I plan to deliver. I
turning down work – I don't think I'm quite ther

Alan Lazar *(Sex and the City, American Cri*
Princess Switch: Switched Again, Holiday ir

I thank my lucky stars every day that I get up an
have somehow avoided having to work in an c
career is always tough, full of ups and down
At the core of it, I think you have to be very pa
work, and you have to truly believe that you j
happy life doing anything else. That passion w
and downs. Then, of course, there's the work
your laurels. Every new project you tackle has
new inspiration, new creative techniques, and
that's never done before, so your work is al
passion is just the starting point. Film, TV, a
really work in isolation. They need to be hi
studios, and networks, and so relationships
working. Relationships with key collaborators n
and develop over many years as one builds de
and a shared history of joy in projects you've
my US career by attending USC Film School,
directing. I started writing music for some of
and realized this was where my true passion
the 25 movies or 30 TV shows I've worked on
I got going back in film school. Film school a
of filmmakers. I think communicating with film
needs and converting them into the deep emo
huge part of the job. The music is always seco
there to support character, plot, pace, and the
    The third thing I would add is a more phi
very frustrated in the early days of my career

soon realized that most of my most rewarding
unexpectedly and seemingly out of thin air. I
of the Tao Te Ching, and I meditate daily now.
n being completely unattached to the results of
s to approach this career and avoid heartache.
er door opens. You move one step back and
r next creative project is always waiting there
d of immediate vision. When one opens one's
of this strange road, it becomes a joyful one to

olm X, Eve's Bayou, Love & Basketball,
e Princess and the Frog)

think of:

ft. Find experiences that will help you to grow
ve in other endeavors will broaden your musical
rpen your skills, which could bring something

t's the hard one for me. You need to be working
e as an assistant, or whatever it would take to
in my band started playing my themes back to
Immediately, I saw his interest and suggested
ut. He did them without ever coming to me to
lone the research. Once I found out about his
nt, I tried him on a few projects. He then went
projects!

res for Journey, ABZU, Assassin's Creed
ja 1-3, The Pathless, LEGO Fortnite, Stray
cal)

fantastic, deeply pragmatic advice for young
p-line pros, and I can heartily affirm just about
nowing those bases are covered, I think the
r composers is to remember to get out of your
hose inconvenient bursts of inspiration in the
ut I think we all too rarely stop to think why that
vriting your own, seems to live simultaneously
bconsciousness, and letting that latter domain

cook is a powerful tool. It took me far too m
this, as a workaholic chained to his desk who f

But it's about more than just letting ideas s
There are thousands and thousands of talente
great gear all over the world. So what ends u
make YOU able to carve out your own space
point of view and the way that comes throu
enrich that point of view with as much life expe
and think why you love the music of [insert cc
the Williams, Goldsmiths, Zimmers, Elfmans
Greenwoods, Skrillexs, Glasses, Richter, etc of
are inevitably interesting people, who have stc
music itself and more about them channelin
merely the vessel.

It's really important to spend an enormc
your craft, but don't forget to balance that with
the music that comes out of you is decidedl
adventure, heartbreaks, losses, and victories c

Bill Brown *(Tom Clancy's Rainbow Six,*
Incredible Hulk: Ultimate Destruction, Capt
CSI: NY, Dominion, The Devil's Tomb, Infam

Here is a little additional advice from an intervi
College of Music:

1. How can a young composer become a be
Knowledge is so powerful in composing for m
Read something and write something every da
Look at life from a learning orientation always
everyone you meet. It will serve you so well!

a. Watch and study films (DVDs with directo
    are great for learning!)

b. Listen to and study film music (in and c
    orchestral scores.

c. Write music for an emotion or write a suite
    genre as an exercise. Share them with yo
    film makers that are also just getting sta
    social media and in film schools around ye
    genuine - the friends you make early on ca
    in your career! Ask them how your music

า a neutral place without attachment. Always
eady for new ideas to happen. Being a great
ommunicator is a big part of storytelling. Your
ust of your director, and that happens through
them, understand their vision, and elevate the

rn to communicate in dramatic terms instead
about your music in terms of what it's doing
now you communicate with your director when
beyond.

osers develop their compositional palettes?
ever stop exploring, learning, playing, and
to all types of new music and see what
onates with your soul as an artist. *For me, when
ern composers (like Hindemith, Shostakovich,
) in my first year at Berklee, I was just floored.
nusic of my own soul. The only other times I felt
ic.

is business, you need to be ready for anything.
, learn new instruments, learn orchestration,
s, and practice creating music in those styles.
r learning process. Set goals for yourself. Set
ss and journey. Write them down! Write down
career to look like. Even take it a step further
such as, "I am writing awesome music in my
e, inspiring projects with wonderful, creative,
I'm so grateful!"

poser need to know in terms of technology

e Logic Pro or Cubase to start.) Become an
their shortcuts and tools – this will help a
er in lots of ways! Never stop improving your

d sample libraries as you can (Study YouTube
expert! And always stay up to date with the

s. Compare your mixes with professional

127

4. How can a young composer practice film

a. Find young film school students or friends
    making movies and help score them!

b. Make your own film shorts and score them
    expresses your unique voice and persona
    artist!)

c. Practice by re-scoring existing films.

d. Collaborate with friends who are also stud
    orchestration, conducting, etc.

e. Check out the documentary and podcast
    'Perspective (Forum for Film Music)' Facel

5. What are some scores you would recom
be familiar with and why?

*Gladiator, The Last Samurai, The Da Vinci Cc
Knight.* Hans Zimmer has created groundbrea
and continues to this day to recreate the medi

Road to Perdition and *The Shawshan*
Newman (for deep, expressive, unique emotion

Signs and *The Fugitive* by James N
masterclass in scoring, especially with foresha

The Game by Howard Shore: such an
a-tonal score! (And go to Berklee to learn how

Not a score, but: 'GHOSTS I-IV' by Nin
preceded the Oscar-winning score for *The Soc*
and Atticus Ross' continuing exploration into n
hybrid scoring (also check out *The Girl with th*
Watchmen series)

Alexandre Desplat's score for *The Shape*
motivic writing and an elegant use of themes)

And just for fun, check out my score fror
Soundcloud. I had so much fun with that show!
on my website about the process to check out! (

6. How do you make a living as a film comp

I made friends starting early (at Berklee C
friendships are what led to my moving to Lc
scoring games. That led to meeting more
producers in the industry and scoring for mc
and films. One of the directors I met doing a
score a TV film and then a few years later calle

year, an agent called and we started working
er since. Over the next 14 years, I worked on
and even films, consistently sending demos
g my best to get out there and meet more
try. The wider our group of friends/colleagues
ouch, the better chance we have of continuing

vorking, as a professional, in your industry?

re for this job?
tarted 'writing' at 6, fell in love with film music
ongs, learned about synthesis, programming,
school (self-taught), graduated with a BA in
g from Berklee College of Music in 1991, and
s before getting my first real gig and moving to
ed version).

ducation?
e! Changed my life. I learned so much during
I fell in love with modern orchestral music and
osition and theory, orchestration, conducting,
film music, song writing, and more - in great
was blessed with friendships that still are with
o served my career in invaluable ways. All of
s to come in my career. And the friendships

r credentials are required for the 'position'

ume is essentially your credits (TV series, films,
nusic for), your experience in the industry, your
your work as an artist outside of the industry.

ou would tell an aspiring composer?

!

out the magic you create musically that is
anyone else; write what you truly love to write!

If you don't fall in love with what you're doing,
either. Enjoy yourself every day because the
to reach. Everything that is worth experiencir
work and grow and evolve as a composer. Do
fun! Start every cue with a new mind, and don'
… it's play. Never forget, composing is a be.
play. Just close your eyes, listen to that music
of the delicious magic that makes up music.

12. What is one of the biggest mistakes y
that then helped you gain experience?

I think two things that can stifle a composer ir
anything is too precious (will they like it? W'
if it's not what they want?) and (2), on the
thinking 'this is not worthy of writing for' (I'r
don't want to write for commercials, cartoon
experience. The director I met doing a *spec* c
most important friend and collaborator of m
fighting with my management about doing co
busy with game soundtracks at the time!

Being too precious with your music ca
Don't second-guess yourself. Listen closel
reflect on and repeat back to them what the
the direction of the project (to make sure you
excited about it. Trust that the music is on
every project start, every composer I've ever
of dread. "Will I even remember how to write r
It's just being human. The music will come
you. The more excited you get about it, the r
the project with your mind, body, and soul,
no such thing as writer's block, really. The
through you. It's your job to open your heart
in whatever ways work for you. And when yo
which you will, remember it's not personal,
a great thing, because more often than no
teach you something, open a new path for cr
of those things are so helpful for us!

Every day is an opportunity to learn more, a
There is nothing exciting about staying in your
is in challenges and the growth that comes f
changes, and it's a gift for us as artists.

KE EXCUSES OR EXPLANATIONS WHEN
C TO THE CLIENT. It's unnecessary and

your biggest accomplishments in your

hances and stretch out of my comfort zone. I
ng a video game when I started back in 1996,
nce, and it was an amazing, joyful, epic, and
es to be. When I started scoring my first TV
ance in the middle of the first season and left
or at Soundelux DMG, building a home studio
any. It was one of the best choices I've ever
got an email from a touring company based
performing my music from Lineage II live. I
cted live and had never been to Russia, but
es. It took almost a year of preparation, and
one of the most incredible experiences I've
WAY out of my comfort zone and the whole
cal than I could have ever expected. I put
the universe, or whatever you would call it,
d three intentions going to perform there: to
ny heart with my orchestra, and to share my
for all of the love they have shown me over
isic). Intentions can be really powerful. They
of your life if you get in the practice of living
t.

tricks that beginner composers should

Meet directors, producers, music supervisors,
are also in the early stages of their career. Find
tions about them and their work, be curious,
member that there is no career without those
Be curious about everything in life, always.
of your life. Share your music! Make it easy
o your music. Get creative with it. If you're just
wn images to edit to your music or write music
, photos ... everything you are as an artist and
mystery can be good too. Make it interesting
cial platforms. Play your music live on socials.

Share your creative process. Have fun with it
there'. Also, remember that your collaborators
much as possible about the mediums you're c
the projects in their language – dramatic term
television series, and the emotional narrative
your music and themes to those emotions, ch
the conversations from steering too much into
really serve your creative process, which shou
new possibilities in service of the narrative. Ke
stop learning!

15. Are there any professional books you you in your career?

Check out *How to Win Friends and Influence I*
7 Habits of Highly Effective People, The 5 Es
Assert Yourself, Listen to Others, and Resolve
resources section next for many more book re

16. What is the best part about your job tha

That moment when you're scoring something
time any more and you can feel your soul in wh
You're no longer thinking about it, it's just com
in your heart, your body, it makes you laugh or
I love the challenge of starting something new
Then sharing that with your friends/colleagues
having elevated the film together is the amazi
nothing like it. It's why I am still a composer an

Bill Brown
www.billbrownmusic.com

My Website
https://www.
billbrownmusic.com

TO SAY TOMORROW WON'T BE
UR LIFE?

ce really resonates for me is that I've had that
phone call that takes everything to the next
something you really love, meeting someone
ct on your life, making a positive impact on
someone, accepting help from someone else,
lued in some way. The list goes on. There are
next 'best day of our lives' around every corner,
er it's something magical that we didn't expect
each next moment can be the best? I know it's
he.

ges, no doubt about it. There are many ways
With dread, fear, excitement, hope, anxiety,
are all emotions that we might not be able to
houghts when waking up to help remind us of
en we don't accept uncertainty, it becomes
becomes adventure. Resentment or anxiety
in the past and not allowing the present to be
ment when you wake up to think of one positive
be meditate on that for a few minutes. Maybe
ight now in this moment. Maybe it's gratitude
d years ago, something you learned from, or
el very happy. If we've had an experience like
y it's not going to happen again today? And
ves today if we've done so in the past? Who's

e in each moment and continue to make those
. Just take small steps in a positive direction.
another one of those great days? Why not give
omposing is a beautiful, transcendent form of
y because there is no top of the mountain to
th experiencing is going to happen as you work
mposer. Don't miss it! It can be so much fun!

AFTERWO
RESOURC

Thanks for joining me. I hope this book will b
your unique journey as an artist, and I wish
I've experienced throughout mine.

Before you go, here is an exercise arour
do anytime you want. Take some time for you
go somewhere beautiful in nature, and cons
everything in your life for their gifts (all of it,
or 'bad'). In everything, there is always a lessc
intentions for the coming years. Say them to y
as if you're living them now. Know that you are
that what is meant for you will come and wha
enjoy this time now, every day. Remember, th
ever. Your life is happening *now* (not some
'finally get it right'). Trust your instincts. Many t
one. And don't forget the three most importa
maintaining a career in this business: 1. It's ab
relationships; 3. ***It's about relationships!***

RESOURCES

s:

raltools.

Spitfire Composer Interviews

*https://composer.
spitfireaudio.com/en*

g

e.

v-

Soundtrack Academy

https://soundtrack.academy

novie.

Film Score Monthly

*https://www.
filmscoremonthly.com/daily/
index.cfm*

nd

csound.

Bear McCreary Composer YouTube Channel

*https://www.youtube.com/
user/bearmccreary/videos*

an

*e.com/
FqA*

Thomas Newman Full Q&A, Oxford Union

*https://www.youtube.com/
watch?v=oeHNUJ-hNmE*

an -
ore

*e.com/
odE*

Bernard Herrmann Composer Toolkit (with Andy Blaney's 'Benny' mock-up tutorial)

*https://www.spitfireaudio.
com/bernard-herrmann-
composer-toolkit*

er on
lm
th look)

*e.com/
u4c&lis
3NURH*

Andrew Gerlicher on composing for film (Extended Interview)

*https://www.synthtopia.
com/content/2013/12/
trent-reznor-alessandro-
cortini-extended-interview/*

Isolated Film Scores
https://shorturl.at/DSA5A

Film Scoring Tips
https://filmscoringtips.com/

Film Music Media
https://www.filmmusicmedia.com/

A Set Of Tools to Use in Any Composition
https://www.youtube.com/watch?v=rAOcDMkr49k

Maximize Your Orchestral Compositions by Understanding One Important Concept
https://www.youtube.com/watch?v=SibhcFGY6kM

Orchestral Programming: Day One - Christian Henson
https://www.youtube.com/watch?v=wtwQMlB1Gus

Star Wars - Suite for Orchestra Deluxe Score
https://www.sheetmusicplus.com/en/product/star-wars-3979685.html

out:

uments.com

m

/en/

s.com

.com

uk
om
n

m/store/collections/14

om

om

n

/products
ontent/category/computer-music/software-

m/

Composer Plug-Ins/Gear:

www.musictech.net
https://www.gear4music.com/Music-Software.ht
https://www.noisebug.net
https://www.flux.audio/products
https://www.audiority.com
https://www.apple.com/logic-pro/
https://www.synthtopia.com
https://reverb.com/c/keyboards-and-synths/analc
https://reverb.com
https://www.pluginboutique.com
https://www.kvraudio.com
https://www.softube.com/products
https://www.ehx.com
https://www.strymon.net
https://www.eventide.com
https://www.nomadfactory.com
https://www.facebook.com/BeijerWorkstations
https://www.soundtoys.com
https://www.sonnox.com
https://www.fxpansion.com
https://synthesizers.com/index.html
https://www.bestservice.com
https://zero-g.co.uk/
https://www.fabfilter.com
https://soundiron.com
https://www.izotope.com
https://u-he.com
https://zapzorn.com
https://thecrowhillcompany.com/
https://thecrowhillcompany.com/vaults-free-plug

Hire Session Musicians, Producers and mo

https://www.musiversal.com/

ng
to get
cers

Qqi

**All You Need to
Know About Music
Royalties**

*https://blog.groover.co/en/
tips/all-you-need-to-know-
about-royalties/*

ic
IL
d or

com/
Y

**100 Logic Pro
Tips, Tricks and
Shortcuts - YouTube**

*https://www.youtube.com/
watch?v=KPQ2tKD3-4I*

ulture
t

ne-

**The Society of
Composers and
Lyricists**

https://thescl.com

IVE

rum.
rown/

**Tim Davies – How to
Score**

*https://www.timusic.net/
debreved/how-to-score/*

nds!
.com/

**John Williams'
Top Ten Tips for
Success**

*https://www.youtube.com/
watch?v=o1QciU4Z-_k*

nted
er

class.
immer-
1

Cinemagic Scoring

*https://www.
cinemagicscoring.com/*

Video

ages/

Additional Books/Articles:

How to Win Friends and Influence People, Dale (

How to Win Friends and Influence People in the

The 7 Habits of Highly Effective People: Powerfu in Personal Change, by Stephen R. Covey.

The 8th Habit: From Effectiveness to Greatness,

The 5 Essential People Skills: How to Assert You and Resolve Conflicts (Dale Carnegie Training), b

Scoring to Picture in Logic Pro, by Chris Piorkow

Music for Income: High quality educational tools composers looking to make an income from writ Films, and Video Games – https://www.musicfor

Creative Business Handbook, by Ekaterina popo Alicia Puig and Leila Simon Hayes.

Atomic Habits, by James Clear

Artpreneur, by Miriam Schulman

Guerrilla Film Scoring: Practical Advice from Hollywood Composers by Jeremy Borum

Getting the Best Score for Your Film: A Filmmake Guide to Music Scoring by David A. Bell

A Composer's Guide to Game Music by Winifred

Scoring the Screen: The Secret Language of Film

Creative Strategies in Film Scoring - Audio and Video Access Included by Ben Newhouse

Complete Guide to Film Scoring: The Art and Bu Writing Music for Movies and TV by Richard Davi

SCORE: A Film Music Documentary — The Inter by Matt Schrader and Trevor Thompson

The Study of Orchestration (Third Edition) by Sar

Workbook: For the Study of Orchestration by Sar

Sounds and Scores by Henry Mancini

The Film Music of John Williams: Reviving Hollyw Style (Wisconsin Film Studies) by Emilio Audissin

The Struggle Behind the Soundtrack: Inside the World of Film Scoring (Paperback) by Stephan E.

The Score: Interviews with Film Composers by M

Music for New Media: Composing for Videogame Presentations and Other Interactive Media, Paul

The Guide to MIDI Orchestration 4e, Paul Gilreat

on for the Contemporary
o Writing and Sequencing for the
olo and Richard DeRosa

ng for Small and Medium
n Pullig.

mble, Ken Pullig and Dick Lowell.

i and Matthew Nicholl.

chnique for Music Notation, Mark McGrain

s: A Guide for Media Composers
March 17, 2023 by Shie Rozow

Rings Films: A Comprehensive Account
ok and Rarities CD) by Doug Adams

Wonder and the Sound of
Series) by Frank Lehman

s with Some of Horror's
views] by J. Blake Fichera

the Score (Routledge Music and
on by Frank Lehman (Editor)

dvanced Techniques for Modern Harmony
Pro by mDecks Music and Ariel J Ramos

eading Film Music (Paperback) by Royal S. Brown

posers Talk About the Art, Craft, Blood,
Cinema (Paperback) by David Morgan

livan

Vords (Hardcover) by Ennio Morricone

ife and Music of
C. Smith

res, a Selected
y Hubai

on 4e (Hardcover) by Paul Gilreath

sic Website in Minutes

Organizations):

om

om

ABOUT THE A

Award-winning composer Bill Brown is best knoof the hit CBS series **'CSI: NY'**, composing the
'Dominion', as well as writing and producing
'Wolfenstein', **'Lineage II'**, **'Captain America: S**
Rainbow Six' and many more. He also compose
tour music for **Windows XP**, as well as music for
early in his career. His scores for film include '
Gooding Jr., **'Desiree'**, starring Ron Perlman, the
the emotional war drama **'Mending The Line'**.
Accolades for his music include PCXL Magaz
'Tom Clancy's Rainbow Six', Nine **BMI** awa
Editor's Choice Award. His scores have als
the **British Academy of Film and Televisio**
Audio Network Guild, and more.
In 2018, Bill released **'Dreamstate'**, a pe
combines his passion for analog synths, piar
dreamstateproject.com). In 2019, Bill condu
performing his music from **'Lineage 2'** live in c

Bill resides in Los Angeles and is repres
Fortress Talent Management. www.billbrownm